1 2 3 4 5 6 7 8 9 **10**

THE TECH SET

Ellyssa Kroski, Series Editor

Effective Blogging for Libraries

Connie Crosby

lita

Neal-Schuman Publishers, Inc.

New York   London

Published by Neal-Schuman Publishers, Inc.
100 William St., Suite 2004
New York, NY 10038

Published in cooperation with the Library Information and Technology Association, a division of the American Library Association.

Printed and bound in the United States of America.

The paper used in this publication meets the minimum requirements of American National Standard for Information Sciences—Permanence of Paper for Printed Library Materials, ANSI Z39.48-1992.

ISBN: 978-1-55570-713-2

For Sabrina Pacifici,
who taught me I have much to teach and share with others

CONTENTS

Don't miss this book's companion wiki and podcast!

Turn the page for details.

THE TECH SET is more than the book you're holding!

All 10 titles in THE TECH SET series feature three components:

1. the book you're now holding;
2. companion wikis to provide even more details on the topic and keep our coverage of this topic up-to-date; and
3. author podcasts that will extend your knowledge and let you get to know the author even better.

The companion wikis and podcasts can be found at:

techset.wetpaint.com

At **techset.wetpaint.com** you'll be able to go far beyond the printed pages you're now holding and:

▶ access regular updates from each author that are packed with new advice and recommended resources;
▶ use the wiki's forum to interact, ask questions, and share advice with the authors and your LIS peers; and
▶ hear these gurus' own words when you listen to THE TECH SET podcasts.

To receive regular updates about TECH SET technologies and authors, sign up for THE TECH SET Facebook page (**facebook.com/nealschumanpub**) and Twitter (**twitter.com/nealschumanpub**).

For more information on THE TECH SET series and the individual titles, visit **www.neal-schuman.com/techset**.

FOREWORD

Welcome to volume 10 of The Tech Set.

Nowadays it seems as if everyone has a blog—but not all of them are successful. *Effective Blogging for Libraries* is a complete how-to handbook that provides practical tips and best practices for creating a winning library blog and informs readers about everything from blog posting techniques, to strategies for encouraging comments and dealing with negative feedback, to effective tagging. The book tackles approaches to blog marketing, managing staff bloggers, usability guidelines, and a variety of assessment methods. Author Connie Crosby delivers invaluable advice and recommendations for developing engaging blog content, establishing your library's brand, and gaining (and keeping!) readership.

The idea for The Tech Set book series developed because I perceived a need for a set of practical guidebooks for using today's cutting-edge technologies specifically within libraries. When I give talks and teach courses, what I hear most from librarians who are interested in implementing these new tools in their organizations are questions on how exactly to go about doing it. A lot has been written about the benefits of these new 2.0 social media tools, and at this point librarians are intrigued but they oftentimes don't know where to start.

I envisioned a series of books that would offer accessible, practical information and would encapsulate the spirit of a 23 Things program but go a step further—to teach librarians not only how to use these programs as individual users but also how to plan and implement particular types of library services using them. I thought it was important to discuss the entire life cycle of these initiatives, including everything from what it takes to plan, strategize, and gain buy-in, to how to develop and implement, to how to market and measure the success of these projects. I also wanted them to incorporate a broad range of project ideas and instructions.

Each of the ten books in The Tech Set series was written with this format in mind. Throughout the series, the "Implementation" chapters, chock-full of detailed project instructions, will be of major interest to all readers. These chapters start off with a basic "recipe" for how to effectively use the technology in a library, and then build on that foundation to offer more and more advanced project ideas. I believe that readers of all levels of expertise will find something useful here as the proposed projects and initiatives run the gamut from the basic to the cutting-edge.

Connie Crosby has been speaking and writing about emerging technology in libraries for many years and has been blogging since 2004. I knew that if anyone in the field could offer sage advice about the practicalities of creating a sensational library blog it was Connie. If you've been struggling with where to go next with your library blog or are just considering launching a blog initiative, this is a book you won't want to miss.

Ellyssa Kroski
Information Services Technologist
Barnard College Library
www.ellyssakroski.com
http://oedb.org/blogs/ilibrarian
ellyssakroski@yahoo.com

Ellyssa Kroski is an Information Services Technologist at Barnard College as well as a writer, educator, and international conference speaker. She is an adjunct faculty member at Long Island University, Pratt Institute, and San Jose State University where she teaches LIS students about emerging technologies. Her book *Web 2.0 for Librarians and Information Professionals* was published in February 2008, and she is the creator and Series Editor for The Tech Set 10-volume book series. She blogs at iLibrarian and writes a column called "Stacking the Tech" for *Library Journal*'s Academic Newswire.

▶

PREFACE

Blogs allow people to communicate with each other over the Internet at any time. The intended readership can range from a single person sitting home alone to a large class full of students or a community dispersed geographically around the world.

Writing a blog (originally known as a "Web log") is easy. With a little bit of training, anyone can put a blog together. This simplicity is also a major setback. The Internet is overloaded with blogs from anyone, spanning a spectrum from current fashion trends to blogs about the daily activities of the neighbor's cat. As blogging and the "blogosphere" reaches its tenth year, bloggers are finding it more and more difficult to get noticed and maintain readership—readers are just too overloaded with content.

Effective Blogging for Libraries is a one-stop resource that will provide you with the techniques necessary to start and maintain a successful library blog using the most effective, current best practices. You will learn how to choose the best blogging templates to attract and keep readers, while effectively broadcasting your message to your target audience in the most far-reaching way. Importantly, this book not only covers what works, it also discusses things that don't work: questionnaire responses from over 125 different libraries from around the world about their blogging experiences will set you on the right track toward creating the perfect blog . . . and avoiding common pitfalls. You will also find information on all the supplementary Internet programs and services that will boost your blog's readership.

▶ ORGANIZATION AND AUDIENCE

Chapter 1 covers blogging basics, including a discussion on purpose and strategy and discovering audience types and needs. We will look at using the blog to contribute to your library's image, reputation, and overall brand; fostering a sense of community with your blog; and integrating blogs into an existing PR agenda. We will also look at the wisdom on risks and rewards that came out of the blogging libraries questionnaire.

Chapter 2 gets you started on planning your blogging initiative. Here I advocate a team approach where possible, provide ideas on involving staff, discuss implementing a comment policy, and finally review the choices available for selecting blogging platforms (software).

Chapter 3, the real heart of the book, is the practical section you will hopefully refer to again and again in your daily blogging. Not only does it provide information on how to implement a new blog, including considerations in design, layout, and navigation, gaining readership and keeping it, and launching the blog, but also plenty of tips and tricks for finding and creating content, even when you have run out of ideas.

Chapter 4 covers marketing techniques for getting the word out about your new blog, including traditional and newer social media techniques for marketing, as well as a few of the old "analog" methods that of course still work.

Chapter 5 covers blogging best practices, with a particular focus on the lessons in effective and ineffective blogging practices that emerged from the blogging libraries questionnaire.

Finally, Chapter 6 covers ways to analyze and measure the success of your blog, with discussion of which measures are most important and how to track the conversations you initiate.

The book concludes with a helpful glossary and a list of recommended resources packed with suggested readings plus helpful blogs and other Web sites to inspire you.

I have given you many library blog examples throughout the book to introduce you to the spectrum of possibilities. If you would like to see more, I encourage you to also visit the book's companion wiki.

Effective Blogging for Libraries will help you create a blog that is effective and useful. This book was written for everyone who has to work on a blog, no matter the type of library. Administrators will learn how blogging fits into their library's infrastructure, while those tasked with creating the blog will find useful and practical implementation guidance and tips. You may read the book from cover to cover or jump around as needed. Soon, you will be formulating your own best practices and realizing the maximum potential benefit that blogging has to offer. I wish everyone as wonderful an experience blogging as I have had!

ACKNOWLEDGMENTS

I am humbled by the many people who have influenced me over my library and blogging careers, both online and in person. Allow me to thank a few specifically.

First, I must thank Sabrina Pacifici, the "godmother" of law library blogging, to whom this book is dedicated. She has shared so much with me personally and professionally, my career would not be where it is today without her.

I sincerely appreciate the encouragement from my colleague on the "left coast," Steve Matthews. Together with Simon Fodden and Simon Chester, we make up the dedicated administrative team behind the law blog Slaw.ca. I thank Steve for getting me mixed up with this unlikely crowd.

A chance meeting on a flight in 2007 introduced me to Rebecca Jones and a new gig: teaching social networking tools to information professionals at the Professional Learning Centre, Faculty of Information, University of Toronto. Since then, Eva Piorkowski at the PLC has taken a personal interest in my growth as a teacher and consultant, always egging me on to learn and teach more.

I thank my podcasting partner-in-crime, fellow "Community Diva" Eden Spodek, who opened my eyes to the PR perspective on social media. Many of our conversations are reflected in the pages of this book.

Thanks to Patrick Donoahue, whose Web Site Implementation and Management course introduced me to the concept of accessibility, and to Glen Farrelly, who helped me better understand accessibility issues and resources.

I thank Rob Hyndman, who kindly shared words of wisdom and legal advice, and who is a brilliant blogger and social media thought leader in his own right.

It was Ellyssa Kroski who had the vision for this Tech Set series, and I thank her for inviting me to participate alongside such a stellar group of library colleagues.

Martin Gravel also deserves my appreciation—he has always quietly supported me from the wings, and encouraged me to reach higher.

Thanks also go to all my library colleagues, my blog readers, and the many librarians from around the world who took part in the blogging libraries survey for this book. This book is for you! I hope you find it useful.

▶1

INTRODUCTION: BLOGGING BASICS

- ▶ **Definition and Characteristics**
- ▶ **Purpose and Strategy**
- ▶ **Audience Types and Needs**
- ▶ **Risks and Rewards**

Welcome to the wonderful world of blogging! You may have been reading blogs for a number of years, perhaps commenting on some or even written your own. As with any technology, blogs have evolved through the years. Today's blogs bear little resemblance to the originals. Before we jump into the details of planning, creating, and administrating a library blog, let's look at the blog universe (or "blogosphere") to get some context for embarking on your exciting new project. Keep in mind there are a lot of different things you can do with any given blog. Therefore, take the steps one at a time. You do not need to do everything described in this book; be selective. Choose those features, tools, and marketing methods that fit into your overall strategy. It is preferable to keep things streamlined and elegant rather than cluttered and complicated.

▶ DEFINITION AND CHARACTERISTICS

On a basic level, a blog is a Web site that is easily updated with new messages. These messages, or blog posts, can be brief or long, but they automatically appear on the site arranged together in order of date with the most recent at the top. Blogs were originally written by one person and therefore presented one point of view, but many of today's popular blogs have a number of contributors and represent a range of viewpoints typically focused around a central subject.

Some of the software platforms used for blogs are so dynamic, and at the same time so easy to use, that they are being used for full Web sites. Many of these Web sites do not even look like blogs but allow the Web site owners to easily update the content even when they have little technical knowledge (see Figure 1.1). WordPress and Squarespace are two platforms that allow easy Web site content management (see Figure 1.2).

▶ Figure 1.1: The Yale Arts Library Blog (http://artslibrary.wordpress.com) on WordPress

▶ Figure 1.2: Sara Kelly Johns' Library-Related Blog From the Inside Out (http://fromthe insideout.squarespace.com) on Squarespace

There are also content management systems (or CMSs) that include blogs as one of their tools. Open source CMS Drupal (http://drupal.org) is often used for blogging, and MS SharePoint and Microsoft Office SharePoint Server (MOSS; both from Microsoft—see http://sharepoint.microsoft.com) include the ability to set up blogs as well as wikis.

Typically, blogs have the following characteristics (see Figure 1.3):

- ▶ Frequent posts are made, compared with other types of Web sites.
- ▶ Posts are in reverse chronological order.
- ▶ Date and time are indicated on individual posts.
- ▶ Older posts are lower on the page or "archived" to another page.
- ▶ A calendar or date list is included, giving access to past archives of posts.
- ▶ Titles are given for each individual blog post.
- ▶ Author name where more than one author contributes to the blog is included.
- ▶ Comments can be made on individual blog posts by readers.
- ▶ A related feed for the blog is included so that people can monitor new posts using feed readers such as Google Reader or Bloglines (more about this later).

In Figure 1.3, we see the John Oxley Library Blog from the Queensland Government Web site. In this case the archive of past blog posts is given as a dropdown menu and listed by month. Recent blog posts are available from the left sidebar.

Over time other features have been added to blogs. We will explore many of these throughout the book. Pick and choose what best suits your library's needs. It is advisable to keep things as simple as possible while still accomplishing your goals so that both your blog authors and readers can easily find their way around and use the blog.

▶ PURPOSE AND STRATEGY

Why are you considering starting a blog on behalf of your library? Just because everyone else is doing it does not mean you should. A blog is just one tool in your larger toolbox of communication tactics. Think about your target audience, which community or communities you want to reach, and whether a blog is the suitable vehicle to reach them. Look at your organizational mandate and strategy, and determine if a blog correctly aligns with them.

▶ Figure 1.3: The John Oxley Library Blog (http://blogs.slq.qld.gov.au/jol) with Typical Blog Features Indicated

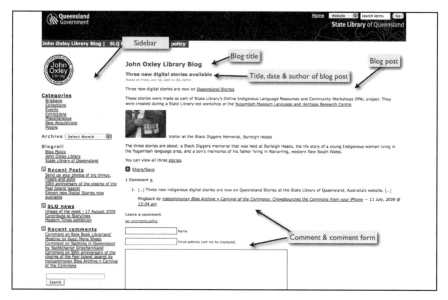

Use Your Blog to Brand Your Library

You may be trying to build your library's image, reputation, or brand. Or perhaps you are trying to rebrand your library. While your library's main Web site may have a professional or even impersonal feel, a blog can bring out your library's personal side. It can show some of your fun-loving internal culture or express how dynamic and cutting-edge you really are. A blog can also highlight staff personalities, especially someone who is charismatic or a thought leader. Let the blog show the community your expertise!

Be careful, however, not to hang your brand on one personality. Someone smart and exciting could very well leave your organization, and then you are left starting over. Better to showcase a few individuals or a team if you have any say in the matter.

Join the Blogosphere Conversation

Having a blog allows for you to join existing conversations in a few ways:

▶ It provides a place for discussion to take place; without a place to talk, your clients or patrons may be holding the conversation about your library someplace else.

▶ It gives you a vehicle to respond to conversations that are elsewhere.

▶ It lets you initiate new conversations independent of time or location.

Who exactly are you talking with in all these conversations? It could really be anyone, but ultimately your focus should be on drawing in those from the community or communities you are serving. You therefore need to think about the types of issues that would interest them. You not only want to get them thinking about specific issues, but also you want to engage them in conversation and ideally have them drop by in person to your library or contact you to use your services.

Foster a Sense of Community with Your Blog

Sharing related events—either online or in person—can help build and engage a community. You want to get people talking not only to you but also to each other. A blog can give them a place to do this if you attract people who are willing to comment. Not everyone is comfortable commenting on blogs, and some groups tend to be more comfortable than others. Consider whether a forum (with threaded posts) or a Facebook page would better suit your needs to engage your community. Oddly enough, library staff tend to be reluctant to comment on blogs. If you are going to create a blog for community building, this is a fear you and your fellow library staff may have to overcome!

Think about using the blog to advertise events, cover upcoming events, describe the event and discussions that took place, and extend the discussions about issues coming out of the events. You can also feature people in the community, as well as their organizations and what they are doing. Perhaps there is a pressing topic in the news that they should be made aware of. You may even want to get involved in advocacy, making your blog a vehicle for giving the community a voice when they are oppressed and urging governments or other bodies to make changes.

There are some who say that you don't create communities, you join them. This is true, but I believe libraries can be an excellent catalyst for bringing people together and helping them find their real community, whatever their interests. Using a blog or other online tool can help you achieve this if you put some real compassion and commitment into your community.

Integrate Blogs into an Existing Public Relations Agenda

Some see blogs as marketing; however, those blogs that push out just one consistent message tend to get boring quickly and are not read. Instead, truly successful and effective library blogs are about public relations (PR) and two-way communication. If you think about blogs for branding, joining the conversation, and community building, you see that these are all methods of good communication and PR.

These guidelines will help you reach and keep an audience:

▶ Don't just make the blog about pushing your services or resources. Do mention them, but don't make that the focus.

▶ Keep it conversational. Let your readers know there is a real person or real persons blogging.

▶ Respond to questions and concerns that come up in the comments or other feedback you get in the blog.

▶ Encourage all kinds of discussion, not just positive comments.

▶ Let your bloggers be creative and find unique ways of expressing themselves.

▶ Read other blogs and other sites for current topics, ideas, and trends that you may want to incorporate into your own blog.

▶ AUDIENCE TYPES AND NEEDS

Before you start a blog, or even finalize your overall communication strategy, think about who you are trying to reach. Blogs do not appeal to everyone, and some audiences that are avid blog readers do not necessarily comment on blogs.

To help me figure out what might appeal to a certain group, I like to use the Social Technographics Profile Tool from Forrester Research, currently available on their Groundswell Web site (www.forrester .com/groundswell). This tool was created in conjunction with the 2008 book *Groundswell* by Charlene Li and Josh Bernoff. In the book, Li and Bernoff describe levels of engagement with social technologies such as blogs. Their initial research is based on demographic surveys broken down by geography, age, and sex, and the Profile Tool helps interpret these data. Let's look at this in a little more detail.

Blog Demographics

The Groundswell Web site talks in terms of "customers" and "consumers," but what they have to say applies just as well to library patrons or clients. While they talk about "markets," we might relate this to groups or communities we wish to reach. They have classified consumers who are on the Internet into six levels of participation:

1. **Inactives**: Do not create or consume social content (25 percent of U.S. users).
2. **Spectators**: Consume the social content created by others, such as blog posts, user-generated videos, podcasts, music, forums, and reviews (69 percent of U.S. users).
3. **Joiners**: Maintain a profile and connect on social networking sites such as Facebook (35 percent of U.S. users).
4. **Collectors**: Organize content for themselves or others using RSS feeds or tags and like to vote on sites such as Digg (www.digg.com) (19 percent of U.S. users).
5. **Critics**: Respond to the content created by others by commenting on blogs, participating in forums, editing wiki articles, posting ratings, and writing reviews (37 percent of U.S. users).
6. **Creators**: Create social content by writing blogs, publishing Web pages, writing and posting articles, and making and uploading audio and video (21 percent of U.S. users).

These levels overlap. Some collectors will also be joiners; some creators will also be critics, collectors, or joiners. This accounts for the percentages exceeding a 100 percent total. Fortunately, reading blogs hits across most levels. Not all groups will add comments to blogs, however, because that is a higher level of participation (groups that may be classified as Critics).

The Profile Tool shows the breakdowns by age, country, and gender as well. If you are in Canada trying to appeal to 18-year-old males, for example, you will find that:

▶ 12 percent are Inactives.
▶ 74 percent are Spectators.
▶ 63 percent are Joiners.
▶ 19 percent are Collectors.
▶ 29 percent are Critics.
▶ 26 percent are Creators.

You would expect, therefore, this group to leave fewer comments on your blog than the general U.S. user but be slightly more likely to read your blog.

We all hope that our blogs will start a grand conversation; however, we can see from the research done for *Groundswell* that fewer people actually talk on the Internet than read.

Consider Other Communication Vehicles

Think about your audience:

▶ Would they prefer to receive their news via a Facebook group? Younger people may prefer to connect with you personally on Facebook rather than joining your group.

▶ What about a newsletter? Those over 55, for example, tend to be high in the Inactives group. Perhaps a newsletter on your Web site or one sent to them by e-mail would suit them better. If you live in a remote rural area with poor connectivity to the Internet, perhaps a paper newsletter would be better.

▶ A podcast may appeal to some. Podcasting is a lot more work than a blog because it involves creating content, recording, and editing the audio. Podcasts can be pushed out to listeners via both iTunes and a blog page on your Web site.

▶ Video is increasing in popularity, and some public libraries are experimenting with getting their message out via YouTube. This takes even more planning and likely means you cannot get new content out as often. This does appeal to a younger demographic.

It is not always a matter of choosing one or the other venue. Use a number of methods to reach your audience, including blogs. After all, according to the Pew Internet & American Life Project's 2008 research (www.pewinternet.org/Commentary/2008/July/New-numbers-for-blogging-and-blog-readership.aspx), 33 percent of Internet users read blogs, with 11 percent doing so on any given day. Combined with other methods of communication, this can be a powerful way of reaching people.

▶ RISKS AND REWARDS

A questionnaire I sent out to libraries in October 2009 received feedback from 81 libraries with active blogs and 7 libraries that previously had blogs. The questionnaire asked them what worked, what did not work, and what kind of time commitment the blog required. Risks identified include balancing the amount of time spent on the blog with the value (or reward) received in return; and getting others to support the blog project initially, including management, IT departments, Webmasters, and other staff members in the library or the library's parent organization. Some found it not uncommon for others to call the project a "time waster" or to not give it priority; and others did not adequately plan for the blog. Some library staff members start a blog as part of a course requirement, for example, but abandon the effort once the course is finished. One librarian noted the blog she had started was not the correct vehicle for what she was trying to achieve.

Time Spent

The time needed to create and maintain a blog is probably the greatest area of concern for most. Planning it, designing it, organizing staff to contribute, and generally getting it started require the biggest time commitment. Time and effort are also needed to convince staff members that they should take part in creating and maintaining the blog.

Once it is set up, however, you can begin to better judge the time you'll need to spend on the blog. Recommended posting ranges from once a week minimum to once a day maximum, and the time spent on individual blog posts varies from a few minutes (generally between 10 and 30 minutes) to a few hours (about 5 hours a week). Simply re-posting information can be quite fast. Writing longer essay or thought-leadership types of posts takes significantly more time. A few noted on my questionnaire that locating appropriate images such as photographs was often the most time-consuming part of creating a post.

It helps to make the blog part of the staff's job and have them schedule a specific time for posting. One head librarian from a government library pointed out, "If the blog generates a lot of interest, it is going to be more of a time commitment to maintain."

Rewards

Rewards come in two flavors: benefits to your organization and benefits to the individuals involved. Knowing the possible benefits to your organization can help convince those in management level and possibly other departments who need to help you make the blog a success. The key is tying the need for a blog back to your larger objectives, goals, or business strategy. Some possible benefits for the organization include:

▶ Building stronger relationships with the library's clients
▶ Building relationships with possible future clients

▶ Increasing visibility of the library's collection, staff, and services

▶ Delivering services in a new, more efficient manner, possibly replacing existing communication vehicles such as e-mail messages and newsletters

▶ Fostering a culture in the library that is collaborative and forward-thinking

▶ Showing the library and its parent organization as innovative and dynamic

Some benefits for participants include:

▶ Being part of a positive team project

▶ Building a resource that can be used in their own work

▶ Creating a new way to deliver services that is seen as progressive

▶ Creating an opportunity for direct comment and feedback by the library's clients

▶ Demonstrating their expertise

▶ Becoming better known on an individual basis to the library's clients

▶ Having fun

As you can read, the rewards for writing a blog far outweigh the risks. If you plan out all the steps, implementing a blog for your library should be quick and easy.

▶2

PLANNING

- ▶ **Choose Your Blogging Perspective**
- ▶ **Maintain Your Blog**
- ▶ **Get Staff Involved**
- ▶ **Develop a Comments Policy**
- ▶ **Determine Your Blogging Platform**

There was a time when we could easily try out blogs with little time commitment or risk and if it did not work just quietly delete it. Web site visitors, however, are becoming increasingly sophisticated with higher demands. It is best to spend some time planning in advance and putting forward a more professional effort. Playing with the software in advance is a good idea, but keep these efforts to personal or private projects where possible.

▶ CHOOSE YOUR BLOGGING PERSPECTIVE

If you have gotten this far, you likely have an idea of who will be blogging and about what, so this section introduces some popular and effective types of library blogs. Think about where yours fits and whether your library could benefit from any of these perspectives.

- ▶ **Library director's voice**: Directors frequently want to be the main representative of the organization and so may be a likely candidate to author your blog. Keep in mind, though, that due to busy schedules, staff assistance may be needed.
- ▶ **Librarian blogger**: One of the best-known types of library blogging is the individual librarian talking about the library industry, personal learning, events, and his or her own thinking, a blog that is usually independent of the library itself.

▶ **Public library blog**: Some libraries create one blog devoted to library services, and others create blogs for specific audiences, genres, or subject areas.

▶ **Teen- and youth-specific blogs**: As part of a movement in public libraries to attract teens and other youth into the library, and especially to reading, some libraries write blogs specifically for them to talk about events, game nights, summer reading programs, contests, and so on.

▶ **The reference desk blog**: Blogs from the reference desk can cover many different topics, and the two common approaches are the subject-specific blog and the reference tip and story blog.

▶ **Academic library blogs**: College and university libraries often have blogs talking about library hours, events, exams, and new book acquisitions.

▶ **K–12 schools**: Blogs talk about class assignments, resources, and news from the library.

▶ **Special libraries**: Some libraries are devoted to single subjects, such as law and genealogy, and will dedicate their blogs to those subject areas.

▶ **Friends of the Library groups/library foundations**: Such blogs often focus on promoting book sales, summer reading programs, and other library activities or library funding and services.

▶ **Internal blogs**: Blogs internal to the library help boost internal communications. Some examples are a weeding blog to discuss what has been removed and why, a training blog to discuss what is being taught in library-run seminars, an acquisitions blog to explain buying decisions and purchases, and a professional development blog to share what staff learned at conferences, seminars and courses, or in their own reading.

▶ **The private library blog**: More in the realm of book collecting than libraries, private library blogs are written about private collections from the point of view of a book collector or an individual librarian.

For more details on the blog types as well as illustrations and examples of their use in different library settings, see this book's companion wiki.

▶ MAINTAIN YOUR BLOG

Before you begin, think about how often you will update the blog. You want fresh content as much as possible, meaning you should add new thoughts or information on a regular basis. If you are posting breaking news on a certain topic, you may want several short posts a day. If you are providing longer thought pieces, once or twice a week may be sufficient. According to feedback from my questionnaire filled out by blogging libraries (discussed in Chapter 1), the most effective number is a post a day, with a minimum of once a week. You want your readers to find new content when they visit your site. If they are following your RSS feed with a feed reader, you want them to see you frequently. As well, search engines favor Web sites that have frequent new content, so this is a way to help build a good ranking in search results.

Create a Schedule

Especially if you have more than one person blogging, it is important to create a schedule. For example, schedule each person to post one or two times a week. Try to find times that fit into each person's work while keeping blog posts consistent throughout the week. Be flexible: as your bloggers become used to the process, they may find times that work better for them. Their schedules or responsibilities may also change, so their blogging schedule will need adjusting. If only one person is blogging, consider this person's workflow and possible time constraints to consistently adding new content.

Depending on the community you want to reach, you may wish to have special, more substantial blog posts contributed less frequently; for example, have a specialist write an in-depth column or article once a month. Bringing in a few different specialists will give frequent and substantial content for your readers.

Tip

Configure your electronic calendar to send automatic reminders. If your calendar doesn't have this capability, try Google Calendar (http://calendar.google.com). You might even want to set up a separate account for the blogging schedule so that more than one person can administrate the schedule.

Plan for Absences

What will happen during the bloggers' absences, such as vacation, illness, or when just too busy? Here are some options for absences, both planned and unplanned:

- ▶ Have some posts written in advance to use when needed.
- ▶ Designate a staff member to substitute.
- ▶ Invite a special outside guest to contribute.
- ▶ Post a message in advance to explain an upcoming absence and give an approximate date of return.

▶ For an unexpected absence, such as an illness, post a message to explain this. Readers will be understanding if someone has been taken ill.

If it is a group blog, divide the posting schedule up formally so that others cover the posting commitment. You can also encourage everyone to blog more without specific scheduling. Just take care not to let writing new content for the blog fall through the cracks as time goes on.

Back Up Content

As with any other documents, your content should be backed up on a regular basis in case the Web site has a technical problem and loses your archived posts. Specific methods are discussed in more detail later in Chapter 3, but, for now, be aware that you will need to decide who will do this and how often. If you are hosting the site yourself, and the database is on your network, it may already be backed up as part of your network back-up practices. Confirm this with your technology department rather than assuming it is being backed up.

▶ GET STAFF INVOLVED

Involving staff members with the blog is a terrific way to both help them feel a sense of ownership and lighten the load of producing it by spreading the work over a larger group. While some in your library may be inspired by the prospect of starting a blog, others may be less than thrilled. They may see it as yet another management brainchild designed just to give them more work. Take care to pay attention to the personalities involved as you introduce this new idea. Some may need to be convinced the blog will be a worthwhile use of their time, not just a frivolous activity.

Replace Other Services or Communication Vehicles

When incorporating blogs into your overall communication strategy, look to see what communication and information you are currently producing and which staff members are involved. Can the content be re-purposed for the blog? Or, can the blog replace existing communication vehicles or services outright? For example, libraries often produce a regular newsletter. It is time-consuming to pull content together in every category and have it ready in a timely manner so that the newsletter is formatted and distributed on time. Could some or all of that information instead be posted to the blog as it becomes available, as part of a staff member's workflow, thereby making the blog the more efficient tool?

The staff members involved will need to see the benefit of switching to a blog. Someone who has been creating a newsletter or other communication product for a long time may see it as part of their work identity and may need time to adjust. Rather than immediately dropping the older format of communication, you may want to run both concurrently and help the staff member come to his or her own conclusion that the older format is now redundant and unnecessary.

Run a Test

Rather than committing to a long-term blog, try testing the concept with a limited run of posts. This will help you understand the process and demonstrate your vision to the rest of the staff. It is easier to have them buy into something that is concrete rather than something that is hypothetical. Your idea of what is to go into the blog, after all, may be very different from what they are picturing.

For a test blog, you do not need to spend a lot of time on its look. Focus strictly on content, the audience, and the writing style. You can show it to the intended audience for feedback, or you may wish to keep it under wraps until you have your plans established. In this case, the first posts will serve well as content already on the blog when you do open it up publicly.

You can use the test blog either as the beginning of your longer-term blog or as a formal time-limited project, for example, a blog celebrating Black History Month or the summer reading program. Test out the concept, watch how it progresses, and learn from your trial run for future blog projects.

Use a Cooperative Approach

When we think of blogs we often think of opinions from an individual; however, blogs from groups, or cooperative blogs, are rising in popularity. Also known as a "group blog" or a "team blog," a cooperative blog is especially useful for a library for a number of reasons:

- ▶ There is less pressure on any one individual to create content.
- ▶ There will be more frequent posts, keeping content fresh.
- ▶ The reader will be exposed to a variety of voices and viewpoints.
- ▶ Bloggers tend to inspire one another with regard to ideas for content.

▶ Because the blog does not depend on any one individual, the "show will go on" during someone's absence.

▶ Creating a blog together is, in itself, a team-building exercise that could benefit your staff.

The Robert Crown Law Library at Stanford Law School's Legal Research Plus blog (http://legalresearchplus.com) is written by a team of their Advanced Legal Research instructors. It includes legal research tips, law library news from Stanford and other prominent law libraries, tips for legal practice, information about new legal research services and sources, and discussion about writing skills. Posting takes place at least once or twice a week and often several times a day.

Select Appropriate Team Members

To kick off a cooperative blog, brainstorm on who might make a good blogging team. Are there particular viewpoints you want represented? For example, if you are writing a blog to reach out to youth in your community, you will want the staff working with youth in your library to contribute. Consider inviting a few people who have the same role to gain different perspectives on the same subject. You may also want to invite individuals with unique perspectives. What about your library director? Or perhaps you have an e-services librarian or a subject specialist who teens would find interesting?

Note that not everyone is suited to blogging. Some will not feel comfortable writing for the Web and making their words or opinions public. Others may start blogging with good intentions but not have the motivation to continue. Do not force anyone into the role of blogger.

Before approaching potential team members, think about their required commitments. What will be the subject focus? How often will they each need to post? Will all be given the same mandate, or will they be given different mandates? Will some or all be given specific assignments? Will assignments and mandates be dictated, or will team members be allowed to choose or come up with their own ideas?

The more freedom you give them to choose, the more enthusiastic they likely will be as bloggers. For the reference blog at the Newman Library at Baruch College in New York City (http://blsciblogs.baruch.cuny.edu/newmanreference), they decided, rather than to handpick contributors, to give posting access to all reference staff providing desk, chat, or e-mail reference services. The result is about eight staff members who are motivated to post at least once a month and two or three who post every week.

Keep on Track

Enthusiasm may be high at the beginning, but once the novelty wears off in the sixth month of blogging (or earlier) you may find your bloggers waning in interest, and you will see them posting less frequently as other work becomes pressing. Even with a posting schedule, library staff will be pulled in a number of directions and blogging may become a lower priority. Consider how you will keep things from becoming sidelined. Have an automated, scheduled reminder sent to each person—whether by e-mail or your internal calendar system—to nudge them. Also give one or two people the task of overseeing posting and have them remind bloggers who fail to fulfill their blogging commitments.

Blogging is often a creative endeavor, so be flexible. Allowing someone to post on another day or take a little sabbatical from blogging is sometimes helpful. Periodically reassess your scheduling, and allow people to move their posting days to better fit their workflow. If you are just starting, it may take time for everyone to find a good posting rhythm.

Remember to stay focused with subject matter and content. Periodically assess the posts, and give bloggers a heads-up if they stray too much. It is okay to vary the content somewhat, but if your audience isn't finding what they expect, they'll go elsewhere for it.

Keep Staff Interested

Ensure the lines of communication in the blog group stay open. Encouraging discussions about new directions for the blog or solving a problem helps everyone feel connected to the project. Whether these discussions are in person, via conference calls, online, or through e-mail, keep everyone talking and connecting.

There will be times when someone is just not inspired and needs some good content suggestions. Find a place for the group to post links and share ideas that others can use. Encourage everyone to think ahead and jot down ideas even when they don't need them to fill their own "quota." Ideally, your bloggers will feel comfortable asking one another directly for suggestions.

Here are some ways to help your blogging team feel connected:

▶ Celebrate blog milestones and (hopefully) awards.
▶ Occasionally provide a special subject to address as a group, such as a specific theme or an upcoming event.

▶ Hold brainstorming sessions to come up with new blog post ideas or ways to improve the blog.

▶ Thank the team as a whole with a special group event.

As much as possible, foster a culture of creativity and openness. Allow people to experiment with their blogging. This may sometimes be successful, sometimes not; however, this is another way to help keep your bloggers motivated.

Conduct Research for Posts

Even if a staff member does not want to put his or her face publicly on the blog, there are still other roles to be played. Many bloggers have ideas for new posts but do not have the time to both conduct research for related information and to write. Having someone conducting research behind the scenes can be very helpful.

Research for blogs, as with any other research, needs to be accurate and current. The information given in blogs is not expected to be as comprehensive as, say, in an academic paper. For blogs, researchers should look for links to original source material. For example, if your news story mentions a new report, make a link to the report itself. Search for and provide links to other blogs as well that have covered the same subject.

Monitor the Blogosphere

Another essential role is someone who monitors the "blogosphere" (or grand universe of all blogs) as well as the Internet generally to see whether your blog or individual blog posts get any mentions. Having one person centrally monitor for all mentions means you will not have a number of people duplicating the work. Search for trackbacks—links that are created from a blog making the comment back to your blog post. In addition, set up search tools, such as Google Alerts, to find links and mentions. When you find mentions, it is often appropriate to thank the person publicly (such as in the blog comments) for them. It is generally best for the person who made the original post being referenced to respond on another blog.

Respond to Feedback and Comments

In addition to monitoring what goes on in the larger blogosphere, you also need to keep a close eye on the feedback you receive via e-mail or feedback forms, as well as comments posted to your blog. Having one designated person to do this is a good idea. If the comments on your blog are particularly active, you may need a skilled person to diffuse heated discussions and ensure that spam comments do not take over.

Monitor Metrics

Keeping track of the statistics related to the blog, such as number of visitors to the site and number of comments received, is important to demonstrating your success. This task should be added to someone's list of responsibilities, not left to chance. Metrics need to be monitored on a regular basis, not just once or twice a year. Chapter 6 explores monitoring metrics in detail.

▶ DEVELOP A COMMENTS POLICY

You need to decide how you will handle comments. Will you allow them or not? This is where discussions with senior management often get bogged down. There is a good chance they will view allowing comments as risky. What if something negative is said about your library? What if someone posts something that includes obscene language or is libelous? You need to have your answers ready when making your pitch.

Not allowing comments is a key way to mitigate the risks of a blog, but it unfortunately also cuts off the lines of communication that it is intended to foster. Without comments, a blog becomes just an electronic newsletter. As well, not allowing comments implies your organization is not transparent and has something to hide.

By allowing comments, you conversely imply that your organization is forward thinking and open to discussion. People's comments are also a quick way to find out what they are thinking and to get feedback about your services.

The trick is planning in advance for the negative comments. Ways to help mitigate any negativity that occurs include:

- ▶ Moderating comments
- ▶ Writing and posting a comment policy
- ▶ Designating a person or persons to respond to negative comments
- ▶ Deciding in advance how to respond to negative comments

Moderating Comments

If you do allow comments, I highly recommend that you moderate them. Most blog software includes moderation as an option. This means that comments are held privately for an administrator to review before releasing them to the blog. This gives you a chance to delete or edit any post before it goes "live."

Tips for Moderating Comments

▶ Ensure that your designated moderator(s) will act quickly. Nothing is worse than responding to a blog post and not seeing it posted for several days.

▶ Provide your moderators with guidelines as to what is acceptable in the comments and what should be deleted or edited.

▶ Don't delete or edit unless you really have to. You do not want to be labeled as an organization that censors its community's comments.

Some blog software such as WordPress has the option for you to automatically allow comments from those whose comments you have previously approved. This is a nice feature for those who actively comment, and it will reduce your moderator's workload.

Posting the Policy

Write and post your comment policy visibly on your blog before you start. Putting a prominent link to the policy on the sidebar will encourage people to read and hopefully follow your policy.

The policy will make clear what types of comments are not acceptable. You do not want to delete comments just because they are negative; if your library advocates freedom of speech, everyone should be allowed a say. Instead, look for ways to remove comments based on hate and spam. Also make clear whether profanity will be accepted or not.

The "Disclaimer and Comment Policy" of the Jackson Library at the Stanford Graduate School of Business is a good example. There is a link to it at the bottom of the blog (www.stanford.edu/group/jackson library/blog). Comments are open to all but are moderated by the Blog Manager. Commentary, opinions, and reactions to all posts are welcome. Comments should be civil and on-topic. The Blog Manager may exercise discretion at any time to delete comments deemed uncivil, off-topic, spam, or inappropriate advertisements. The wording is simple and gives the library the discretion to decide what is "uncivil" and "off-topic."

By contrast, the Monterey Public Library's Library Blog Comment Policy is a very specific list of what is acceptable in its blog (www .monterey.org/library/aboutlibrary/blogpolicy.html):

- ▶ Comments should relate to the topic being discussed in the original post.
- ▶ Comments should not contain profanity, racial slurs, or any other derogatory terms.
- ▶ Comments should not contain personal or defamatory attacks.
- ▶ Comments should not contain random or unintelligible text.
- ▶ Reasonable arguments for opposing views are encouraged.
- ▶ A posted comment is the opinion of the poster only, and publication of a comment does not imply endorsement or agreement by the Library Director, Monterey Public Library, or the City of Monterey.
- ▶ This blog is not the place to endorse candidates or a particular stance on a currently active ballot measure.
- ▶ In keeping with an existing City Web site policy, links to Web sites outside Monterey.org are not allowed in posted comments.
- ▶ Comments should not advertise commercial products or services.
- ▶ Comments are subject to the California Public Records Act and will be retained as general correspondence for two years.
- ▶ This comment policy may be revised at any time.
- ▶ The City reserves the right to block or delete comments that violate this policy.
- ▶ Your submission of a comment constitutes your acceptance of this comment policy.

I much prefer the wording of the Jackson Library blog. It feels a lot less restrictive for your readers and yet gives the library lots of discretion for how to handle comments. However, if you work in an organization that is very nervous about the prospect of opening a blog up for comment, something along the lines of the Monterey Public Library may be necessary to ease the senior administrators' minds.

How to Comment

The Create Readers bloggers of the National Library of New Zealand noticed their readers were having difficulty knowing how to add comments to their blog. They came up with "How to comment on the Create Readers blog" (see Figure 2.1). This guide is actually a blog post that walks the reader through posting a comment with screenshots. There is a link to the guide from a prominent place in the blog's right sidebar.

▶ DETERMINE YOUR BLOGGING PLATFORM

Unless you are already using a blogging platform or your library system is tied to an existing platform, such as Drupal or SharePoint, you

▶ Figure 2.1: A How-To Guide for Commenting on the Create Readers Blog from the National Library of New Zealand (http://createreaders.natlib.govt.nz/2007/11/how-to-comment -on-create-readers-blog.html)

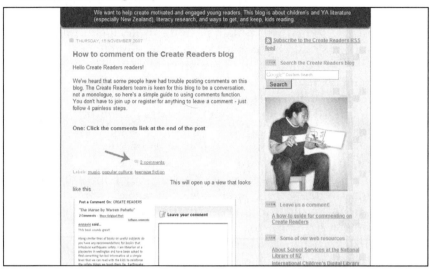

will have to choose a platform. There are a number of platforms already being widely used, so choosing one should not be too difficult. Often the choice comes down to a personal preference for the blog author interface or for the options available.

Hosted versus Self-Hosted

Do you want to host the blog yourself or have someone else host it for you? While most Web sites are hosted outside the organization, it is usually an arrangement wherein the Web site owner has access to the files and databases on the back end. In this discussion, this arrangement—and actually hosting the blog on your own servers—is referred to as "self-hosted." A good example of a Web host that offers this type of arrangement is LISHost (www.lishost.com). It was created by Blake Carver to give inexpensive hosting to libraries. Smaller libraries with few resources may find this a viable self-hosting option.

A number of blog software providers go a step further by also offering hosting, which includes an interface for creating the blog so that access to the underlying files and database of blog posts is not possible. I refer to these as "hosted" blogs. Hosted blogs are quick to set up but mean that the traffic and control of the site will be somewhere else. Usually the biggest objection to having a hosted site is that the domain name is someone else's, such as blogspot.com, typepad.com, or wordpress.com.

Although there is technically nothing wrong with this, it does lend an air of amateurism to the blog. Making the effort to register and purchase your own domain name demonstrates a certain level of professionalism and shows you are knowledgeable about the technology you are using.

This being said, there may be times when you will want to use a hosted solution and not worry about the domain name right away:

- ▶ When you are trying out the software
- ▶ When you are just testing out a new blog concept
- ▶ In an emergency situation where you need to get the word out to people quickly

An example of a blog set up for an emergency situation is the ublaw phoenix blog, created for the University at Buffalo Law Library by Jim Milles when the library experienced a fire in March 2005 and had to move the collection and staff off-site. Library staff posted updates about the collection and photos of the recovery process (see Figure 2.2).

Some hosted solutions such as Blogger will allow you to use your own domain name, so this is becoming less of an issue.

Commercial versus Open Source

Open source software is created by a community of volunteers, many of whom do not meet in person or even necessarily know each other. The community is passionate about the work they do to build the software, and as a result open source packages can often be more advanced with more features than commercial software.

▶ Figure 2.2: The ublaw Phoenix Blog from the University at Buffalo Law Library (http://ublawlib.blogspot.com)

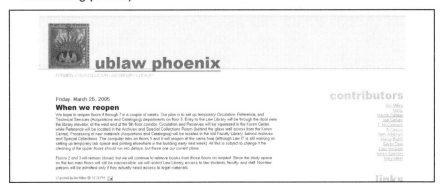

Best of all, open source software is free. Costs, however, can be incurred on the development side. If you don't know how to set up an open source blog, your expenditure goes into hiring someone to set it up and put in the features or plug-ins you need or possibly even create the plug-ins for you.

Organizations often feel more comfortable with commercially produced software unless someone on staff is adept at working with open source codes. Commercial products already have many of the features you need and offer support to help you get started. Squarespace, TypePad, and Movable Type are examples of commercial blog platforms.

Popular Blog Software Applications

Blogger

Blogger (www.blogger.com) is a hosted blog platform owned by Google. It is popular because it is free, is easy to set up, and has a number of features. Blog posts on this platform not surprisingly tend to rank particularly well on Google. You can establish your own domain name or set up a URL on the blogspot.com domain name. Google will sell you your domain name when you first set up the blog if you like.

Blogger has a few templates to choose from, or you can use your own design. Blog owners also have direct access to the underlying HTML code to change things as necessary. For those who aren't coding experts, Blogger has a "drag and drop" feature to rearrange the elements in the template. Some libraries are happy with Blogger, while others do not find it sophisticated enough, especially in its handling of photographs. Some find Blogger to fall short from a usability perspective as well.

If you decide Blogger is right for you, I strongly suggest you use a customized design. The few existing templates have been overused and are starting to look tired. You can hire a designer to create a customized design for you, or look for Blogger templates via a Google search. BloggerStyles (www.bloggerstyles.com), for example, has a wide range of templates and includes a rating system. BTemplates (http://btemplates.com) has a number of free Blogger templates as well.

Drupal

Drupal (http://drupal.org) is an open source content management system with blog capability as opposed to being a blog platform. If you are looking to create a full Web site for your library and not just a blog, using Drupal is one option. With Drupal, McMaster University Library feeds the "Library News" items on the front page of its main Web site from its underlying blog (see Figure 2.3). Drupal is powerful enough to create a robust Web site, but it does require development skills in addition to design work. Blog posts integrate well with other content. This is arguably the most technologically difficult of the options discussed here.

ExpressionEngine

Another content management system that incorporates the use of blog capability, ExpressionEngine (http://expressionengine.com) is used by Web site developers for small- to medium-sized Web sites. This is a commercial application with varying prices depending on organization size and use. There is a free version for personal (noncommercial) and nonprofit use. All levels include the Weblog module. You will need a developer and designer to create the site for you, but this does mean you will get whatever look you want to suit your organization and audience.

The Indiana University South Bend libraries use ExpressionEngine. They created a common look for all their blogs that uses a graphic in the upper left-hand corner to distinguish them (see Figure 2.4). The look is attractive and professional.

LiveJournal

LiveJournal (www.livejournal.com) is a free, commercial, hosted blogging site popular with younger (teen and twenty-something) bloggers.

▶ Figure 2.3: McMaster University Library's Library News Blog (http://library.mcmaster .ca/news)

▶ Figure 2.4: One Book, One Campus Blog from Indiana University South Bend (http://ee
.iusb.edu/index.php?/onebook)

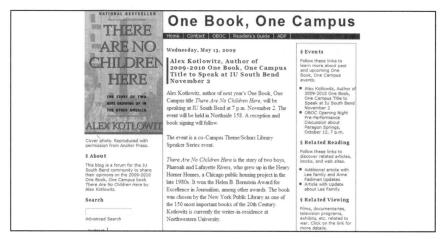

It is also a social networking site, allowing blog owners to connect with their blogging friends. Many use LiveJournal to chronicle their lives. It is not an appropriate platform for most audiences because it is not professional in appearance, but it can have some specific uses. Barnard Library, for example, uses LiveJournal as a way to connect with the 'zine (Internet-based magazines by and for youth) community with its Barnard Zines blog (http://barnardzines.livejournal.com).

If you have been using LiveJournal yourself (in your personal life), then this may be an appropriate choice if you are appealing to a younger audience. Take care, however, not to be that older person trying to look hip. Your younger audience will think you are trying too hard and could see this in a negative light.

Movable Type

Movable Type (www.movabletype.com) from Six Apart has been around for a long time, and those very familiar with it often favor it. It is a commercial blog platform, and the purchase price will depend on the size of your organization and number of bloggers you will have. You must also host it yourself. It can be used inside the firewall of an organization in addition to publicly on the Internet. While not all of Movable Type is open source, it does have a developer community that has created a number of open source plug-ins for it. Some developers even distribute Movable Type with their own plug-ins. This is not an easy platform to work with, but if you have a developer on staff who favors Movable Type, this may be the way to go.

The Binghamton University Libraries Science Library Blog (see Figure 2.5) has the same look as the university's main Web site. It includes a list of blog contributors and their contact information in the right sidebar.

MS SharePoint

Similar in some ways to Drupal, SharePoint (http://sharepoint .microsoft.com) is a content management system or portal platform (two versions are available) that includes blog and wiki capabilities. SharePoint is a Microsoft application and is used extensively inside corporations and other large organizations. The portal version is known as Microsoft Office SharePoint Server or MOSS. If you are in an organization that is running SharePoint, then you have free access to the blog features.

If you are familiar with SharePoint, you may enjoy working with the blog features. For anyone used to other blog platforms, however, SharePoint can seem cumbersome and inflexible because there is a steeper learning curve with this platform than with many of the others.

Todd Klindt is a SharePoint administrator and author who has a rare SharePoint blog (see Figure 2.6) outside the firewall (i.e., publicly on the Internet) that you can view at www.toddklindt.com/blog. It runs like a page (or series of pages) under one tab on his main Web site (www.toddklindt.com).

▶ Figure 2.5: Binghamton University Libraries Science Library Blog (http://library.lib .binghamton.edu/mt/science)

▶ Figure 2.6: SharePoint Blog from Todd Klindt (www.toddklindt.com/blog)

Squarespace

Squarespace (www.squarespace.com) is a commercial, hosted blog platform available on a paid subscription basis. Cost varies depending on functionality and whether you have the Web site on your own domain name or the squarespace.com domain. Squarespace blogs are easier to set up than WordPress blogs but have similar sophisticated functionality. It has a number of templates with a drag-and-drop layout so that the Web site creator does not need to know how to code and a number of plug-ins. You can load in different banners and select different colors for your fonts and sidebars. Designers and developers, however, can still have access to the underlying code and CSS to customize the site.

While Squarespace has been around for a few years, it is not well-known and has started making a name for itself only recently. As a result, libraries have not yet caught on to using it. Library media specialist Sara Kelly Johns' From the Inside Out blog (see Figure 2.7) is an example of a basic layout using Squarespace.

TypePad

TypePad (www.typepad.com) is Six Apart's commercial, hosted option. It is suitable for a basic site but is probably the most restrictive software as far as customization. TypePad has a range of subscription prices, and all levels include support. Thousands of designs are included, and design customization is available at the higher subscription price levels.

Washington University Libraries has a large number of blogs, all based on one TypePad platform (see Figure 2.8). The blogs have a standard look, although some of the looks have been customized. The full list can be found at http://wulibraries.typepad.com.

▶ Figure 2.7: From the Inside Out by Sara Kelly Johns (http://fromtheinsideout .squarespace.com)

▶ Figure 2.8: Math News from the Washington University Libraries (http://wulibraries .typepad.com/mathnews)

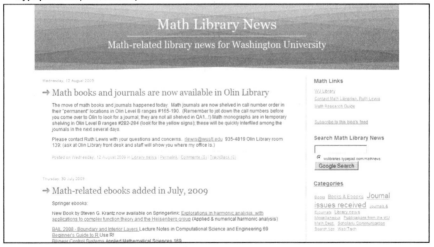

WordPress

WordPress is the best known of the open source blogging software and is used extensively around the world. It can be used as a content management system for a simple Web site in addition to acting as a blog platform. Many devoted bloggers will use only WordPress, as it is flexible, provides a wide range of options, and is frequently updated with new options. For those who are adept at Web development, creating WordPress plug-ins is easy and thus provides a lot of flexibility.

A free, hosted version is available at http://wordpress.com. It has templates (WordPress calls them "themes"), or you can create your own design with CSS. You can use their wordpress.com domain or pay a nominal yearly fee to redirect the site to your own domain. WordPress even provides domain name registration. You are given a generous amount of online storage and can purchase more. WordPress permits up to 35 bloggers to access the site, and again there is an additional charge for more people.

An open source version for downloading to your own host is available from http://wordpress.org. This requires that you have your own Web site host and will install WordPress software. Some Web hosts have simple one-button installation of WordPress, and this is worth asking about. As changes are made to the WordPress platform, new versions are released. Some hosts' setup for WordPress installations will do the upgrade with one simple click of a button. It is advisable to back up the content of your site before doing these upgrades "just in case."

Through an initiative called My Kansas City on the Web, the Northeast Kansas Library System has been working with libraries in Kansas to create good-looking, functional Web sites with WordPress (e.g., see Figure 2.9). The libraries are using WordPress as a content management system to power their whole Web sites. To see other examples, check the list in the sidebar of the Northeast Kansas Library System's main Web site at www.mykansaslibrary.org.

Having learned what goes into planning a blog, you can turn now to the next chapter, which will show you how to implement your plans and create an effective blog.

▶ Figure 2.9: Atchison Public Library Blog (www.atchisonlibrary.org)

►3

IMPLEMENTATION

- ► **Create an Effective Library Blog**
- ► **Enable Ease of Navigation**
- ► **Design for Usability**
- ► **Establish Your Library's Brand**
- ► **Develop Blog Content**
- ► **Launch Your Blog**
- ► **Encourage Participation in Your Blog**
- ► **Deal with Negative Feedback**
- ► **Gain a Readership (and Keep It!)**

► CREATE AN EFFECTIVE LIBRARY BLOG

Blog Design

People are becoming increasingly sophisticated in what they expect to see on a Web site. They expect good design and a layout or structure that is not confusing. They are also less and less willing to wait for a page to load or to function the way they expect.

Good design, therefore, is important. Design elements include color, graphics, layout, navigation, and cohesive fonts. They must all work well together and be neither too busy nor too boring. Many of us (including me) do not have strong design skills. Good design can, fortunately, be achieved in a few easy ways.

Choose Your Template

Many of the blog platforms include free, pre-made templates. Some blog software allows you to adapt them by putting in your own image for the header or to "tweak" the underlying HTML code to change things like font type, size, and color.

Depending on the blog platform you choose, you may also purchase additional templates or have someone custom design one for you. For example, there are hundreds of free WordPress themes in the WordPress.org "Free Themes Directory" (http://wordpress.org/extend/themes). There are also a lot of people who design and sell WordPress themes.

It all depends on your budget, your goals, and how closely you want the blog to tie in with your main Web site or your audience. Make sure you read this book first and decide what you are looking for in a template before you finalize, especially if you are spending money to purchase or have one designed.

Here are some things to consider:

- ▶ Is it compatible with the latest version of the blog software?
- ▶ Is it easy to customize?
- ▶ If you have multiple authors, are authors identified in the individual blog posts?
- ▶ How easily can you add new features to the sidebars?
- ▶ Can you add third-party widgets easily to the blog?
- ▶ Is the date and time of each post shown on the individual posts?
- ▶ If you are using categories or tags (to be explained later), do the categories or tags show in the individual blog posts? On the sidebar?
- ▶ Is there a way to navigate to all previous blog posts?
- ▶ Does it have colors that either match the look you are going for or can be adapted?

It is also a good idea to validate the template code to ensure there are no errors in it before you start using it. WordPress.org has a Validation Checklist to assist you (http://codex.wordpress.org/Validating_a_Website). Also test your template on as many different browsers as possible. See if it is compatible with the current and previous versions of Internet Explorer (IE), Firefox, Safari, Opera, and Chrome. The site BrowserShots (http://browsershots.org) can assist with checking browser compatibility.

Use a Free, Pre-made Template

All of the blog platforms include free pre-made templates, with the exception of Drupal and SharePoint (which you have to build). Some have more selection than others; for example, compared to WordPress's hundreds of themes created by the WordPress community, Squarespace has 60 and Blogger has 16 classic looks with some color variations. Try to find a look that isn't already overused. The Blogger templates have been around for a number of years and not only have been overused but are also looking dated.

Purchase a Template

For some of the platforms you can purchase templates from third parties. WordPress in particular has a large community that creates templates, some of which are free and many more of which are for sale. Search for "premium WordPress themes" to find those for purchase.

Make sure you know what features and functionality you are looking for before you spend money on a template. Otherwise, you may spend a lot of time customizing the template, not achieving what you need, and starting over.

Here are some additional things to look for:

▶ Check whether there is support for the template, in case you run into difficulty.
▶ Does it come with instructions on how to install it and customize it?
▶ If it has photos incorporated into the design, are you given the original photos? This will help you customize the look.
▶ If your blog platform is upgraded, will you automatically receive the upgraded templates, or will you have to purchase them?

Be aware that you will likely have to adapt or tweak your template to some extent. Make sure you take this into account with your budget.

Adapt an Existing Template

Once you have a template, either free or purchased, you can adapt it to give your blog a unique look. You will need access to the underlying HTML code, however, and possibly the cascading style sheet (CSS). You can do simple things like changing the banner and changing the font. Talented designers can do a lot more to change the functionality of an existing template to do exactly what you want. Some benefits are that you do not need to pay someone to design a template from scratch, and you already have an idea of what it looks like. You also know that it is fully functional from the outset.

Create Your Own Template

You can create your own blog look or hire someone to do so. Hiring someone will likely be your most expensive option and possibly the riskiest. However, if you already have a Web design and need the blog to match, this is probably the way to go.

You also run into the challenge of determining the architecture of the site from the beginning, figuring out how things should be laid out. Ideally you create a template that can easily be changed and adapted to suit the changing needs of your audience.

Sidebar Design

Most blogs have two or three columns: the main body and one or two sidebars. The sidebars on a blog can scroll down almost indefinitely. Give some thought as to what you are going to post there and how it is going to look as time goes on and you build up more content, such as links and archived posts.

Keep in mind that people who read your blog through their feed readers won't see your sidebar content. If you do add an essential new item to a sidebar, post a note on your blog with a link back to your site so those readers will learn of the change.

The following sections discuss some of the more essential features to consider for your sidebar. Pick and choose what works with your blog and audience. There are a lot of other features that can be added. Be selective, as you want a clean, professional look. Too many graphics, fonts, and scrolling text will make your blog look too busy and will be a turnoff for most audiences.

Subscribe to the Blog

Your readers should be able to subscribe to your blog in at least one of two ways: by feeds and by e-mail.

One thing that makes a blog a blog is the ability to syndicate the content through a feed. Common feed types are RSS (used by most blog platforms) and Atom (used by Blogger). This allows your readers to see new content through their feed readers (or aggregators) and even allows you or others to pull your blog headlines and posts onto other Web sites. Having a link or button giving access to the feed, then, is essential. There are a lot of different ways to do this, but the orange RSS icon originally created by the Mozilla Foundation (the same people who brought us the open source browser Firefox) has become somewhat of a standard and is likely your best bet. It is available in a number of different formats from Feedicons.com.

The Engineering Library Blog from the NTU Library at Nanyang Technological University in Singapore (see Figure 3.1) has done a

▶ Figure 3.1: The Engineering Library Blog from the NTU Library at Nanyang Technological University (http://blogs.ntu.edu.sg/library/engl)

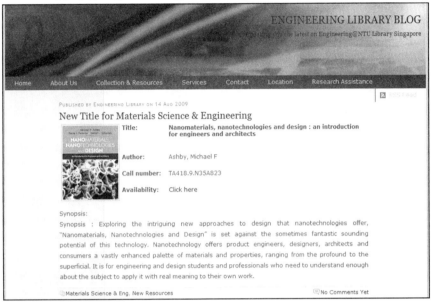

nice job of incorporating the RSS feed at the top of their blog, just under the main banner.

The Utah State Law Library (see Figure 3.2) has a number of blog post categories, each with its own RSS feed. They have grouped them together for reader convenience. For example, readers can view "Library News" or "New Books" separately.

The orange square may be considered somewhat of a standard, but if you have a blog that requires a specific color palette, Feedicon.com also has colored icons in a range of formats. For example, the Canadian law and technology blog Slaw (www.slaw.ca) has an all-blue design, so a blue RSS icon is used.

It may seem counterintuitive to have a blog subscription available via e-mail, but many people are still e-mail oriented and prefer to be notified this way. Depending on your audience, you may want to include this feature. Librarian and author David Lee King has done a nice job of making both RSS and e-mail subscriptions easily accessible from his blog (www.davidleeking.com).

Commonly used tools to create e-mail subscriptions from feeds include the following:

► Figure 3.2: Utah State Law Library Blog (www.utcourts.gov/lawlibrary/blog)

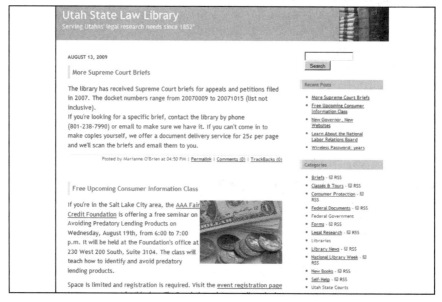

► Google's well-known FeedBurner tool (http://feedburner.google
.com)
► Blog Flux (http://subscription.blogflux.com)
► Feed Blitz (www.feedblitz.com), a slicker e-mail service for a nominal fee

The UK eInformation Group has gone a step further and provides
an RSS feed to comments posted on the blog (http://ukeig.wordpress
.com) in addition to RSS feeds for the blog posts and e-mail subscription. Having a feed specifically for comments is becoming increasingly
popular.

There is no standard place to put subscription links, although most
people expect them to be readily visible either toward the top, likely in
a sidebar, or, less desirable, in the blog footer. I recommend you keep
it visible toward the top. Many templates surprisingly do not include a
subscription function, so you will likely have to add it yourself.

Identify the Bloggers

Especially when a number of people are contributing to the blog, it is
important to identify the bloggers for your readers. One way is to list
them in a sidebar. The names ideally will link to profiles of the
bloggers and to a collection of their respective blog posts. Individual

blog posts should also identify their authors when the blog has more than one.

Avoid anonymous blogging. This may be intimidating at first if your bloggers are not used to writing publicly. However, readers need to know whose perspective is being presented so they can evaluate the content for themselves, just as we evaluate any Web site in our research. Having bloggers clearly identified also lends credibility when they are well-known or high-profile. Finally, identifying your bloggers also shows your organization to be open and honest.

Include Blogrolls/Linkrolls

You may not realize it at first, but starting a blog puts you squarely into a community of bloggers. One way to support other bloggers and also lead your readers to additional good content is to create a blogroll.

A blogroll is simply a list of links to other blogs. Some blogrolls are just a long list of blogs, while others are arranged into categories.

Popular Blogroll Applications

▶ **Bloglines** (www.bloglines.com): This free RSS feed reader has a blogroll-generating feature, whereby the blogs you are following through Bloglines populate your blogroll. I suggest setting up a library-specific or blog-specific Bloglines account just for this purpose.

▶ **Google Reader** (www.google.com/reader): The Google Reader Blogroll Widget tags those blogs in your reader that you want to include in your blogroll. As with Bloglines, you may want to set up a Google Reader account just for your library or your blog, although keep in mind you cannot be logged into two different Google accounts at the same time.

▶ **FeedBurner** (www.feedburner.com): This Google RSS tool has a number of features. BuzzBoost helps you set up headlines from one or more of your feeds, and you can decide how many posts to show from each feed and whether to include an excerpt from the blog posts or other feeds as well.

▶ **Feevy** (www.feevy.com): This free little "dynamic blogroll" tool puts the latest blog post headline at the top of your blogroll so that you have fresh content posted to your sidebar continuously. It currently does not have a lot of flexibility with regard to style—black, white, and "liquid" (no specific width and uses your background colors).

▶ **Delicious** (http://delicious.com): If you want to link to more than just blogs, such as other Web sites and specific resources on the Web, or perhaps show a rotating list of blog posts and articles, then consider using a service such as Delicious to generate a "linkroll."

Some are created by hand, while others are generated automatically with a widget or other code.

There are so many applications for generating or administrating the blogroll that it is difficult to choose one. I searched my favorite social bookmarking site, Delicious, to see which came up as most bookmarked. I include here a list of the top sites, but for more information, setup instructions, and illustrations of these apps, see this book's companion wiki.

Use Trackbacks

If another blog is linking to a specific post on your blog, it is nice to have that piece of the conversation aggregated along with yours. A link back to that post referring to yours is a "trackback" or "linkback" (see Figure 3.3). Trackbacks are sometimes generated automatically; sometimes the blog software requires a special link be added to create the relationship between blog posts.

▶ Figure 3.3: Trackbacks (with Comments) on a Post on Gerrit van Dyk's Shaping Libraries Blog (http://shapinglibraries.wordpress.com)

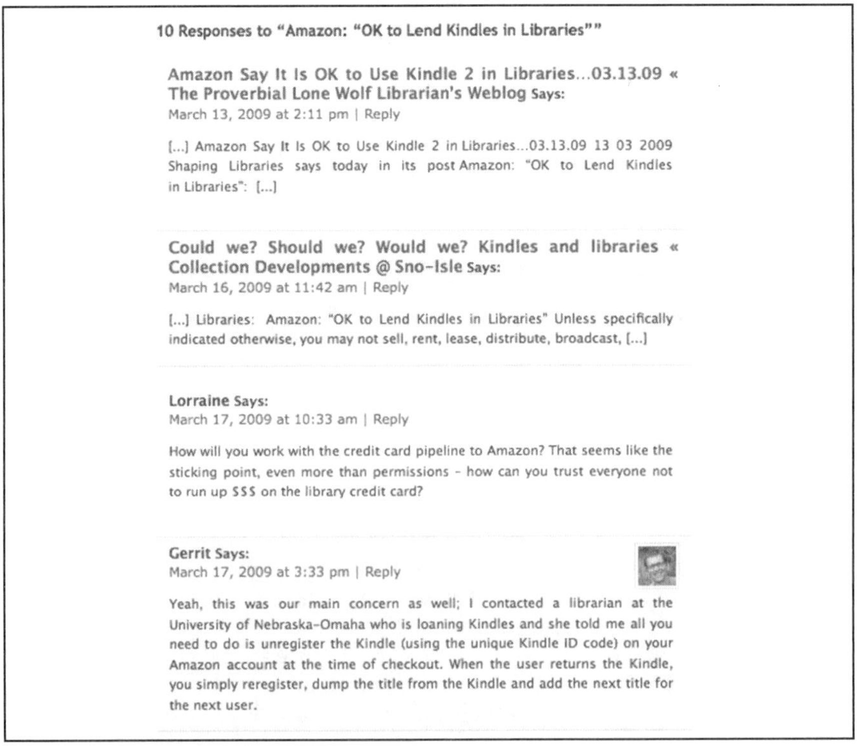

10 Responses to "Amazon: "OK to Lend Kindles in Libraries""

Amazon Say It Is OK to Use Kindle 2 in Libraries...03.13.09 « The Proverbial Lone Wolf Librarian's Weblog Says:
March 13, 2009 at 2:11 pm | Reply

[...] Amazon Say It Is OK to Use Kindle 2 in Libraries...03.13.09 13 03 2009 Shaping Libraries says today in its post Amazon: "OK to Lend Kindles in Libraries": [...]

Could we? Should we? Would we? Kindles and libraries « Collection Developments @ Sno-Isle Says:
March 16, 2009 at 11:42 am | Reply

[...] Libraries: Amazon: "OK to Lend Kindles in Libraries" Unless specifically indicated otherwise, you may not sell, rent, lease, distribute, broadcast, [...]

Lorraine Says:
March 17, 2009 at 10:33 am | Reply

How will you work with the credit card pipeline to Amazon? That seems like the sticking point, even more than permissions - how can you trust everyone not to run up $$$ on the library credit card?

Gerrit Says:
March 17, 2009 at 3:33 pm | Reply

Yeah, this was our main concern as well; I contacted a librarian at the University of Nebraska-Omaha who is loaning Kindles and she told me all you need to do is unregister the Kindle (using the unique Kindle ID code) on your Amazon account at the time of checkout. When the user returns the Kindle, you simply reregister, dump the title from the Kindle and add the next title for the next user.

Provide Contact Info

Nothing is more frustrating than wanting to get in touch with the owner of a blog and not finding any way to do so. It is essential to include your contact information on the blog!

At minimum, include an e-mail address. If you are concerned about spam, set up a separate e-mail box for this purpose; however, make sure this is forwarded to someone and monitored on a regular basis. Some readers may prefer to send comments via e-mail rather than posting them on the blog.

Link to Your Main Web Site

When conducting research for this book, I came across a lot of library blogs that did not link back to their main library Web sites. Don't forget that people can come to your blog via Web searches or direct links. No doubt one of your goals for the blog is to create interest in and use of your library, so don't forget to drive the traffic back to it. A prominent link in your sidebar is key.

Archive Previous Posts

Once your old blog posts fall off the page, what happens to them? Technically they will reside in a database, but how will people retrieve them? Include a search box as well as at least one or two of the following access points, depending on how your blog is set up:

- ▶ A chronological list of archived posts (usually by month)
- ▶ A calendar with links to archived posts
- ▶ Categories with links to past posts that fall within those categories
- ▶ A list of tags with links to posts that were tagged
- ▶ A tag cloud that graphically represents the tags used on your blog

Search may be a feature already available on your blog platform (e.g., Blogger provides a search box at the very top of the page). You can also set up your own search box. For example, you can request the use of Google search on your site. Google has a few different tools for this depending on your needs. For instructions on setting up Google search for your own Web site, check the Google AJAX Search API page (http:// code.google.com/ apis/ajaxsearch).

> For more detailed information on archive access options and illustrations of their use in various library settings, see this book's companion wiki.

Page Design

Some blog platforms, such as WordPress, Squarespace, and Drupal, allow you to create static pages in addition to your dynamic blog. These can be used in any number of ways to keep content "up top" and prominent on the site. This is also what allows you to use the blog as your main Web site if you prefer. A lot of organizations use WordPress, for example, for their Web sites. I use WordPress for my own consulting business Web site, with categories to feed updates to different parts of the site.

The following list provides a few examples of what you can do with pages to supplement the main blog content. Most of these are administrative pages. The pages, then, become a place to park important information for future reference. Links can be made to these pages from the front of the blog as appropriate, and you are not cluttering up your front-and-center space with "administrivia."

For more examples and illustrations of these and other page design options, see this book's companion wiki.

▶ **About Page**: Your readers want to know as much as they can find out about you! Use this page to tell them about your library, the programs they might be interested in, the purpose and focus of your blog, and background on the bloggers. Be sure to build relevant links to your library's main Web site.

▶ **Contact Info**: Include your contact information in a sidebar or as a separate page. Some bloggers prefer on-site contact forms that readers fill out because this helps to reduce spam, but it also prevents people from forwarding files and other attachments and distances you from readers.

▶ **Feedback Page**: If you encourage reader feedback, you can create a page with a simple e-mail form or dropdown menus to direct the feedback to yourself or different people in your library.

▶ **About RSS**: Because the use of RSS feeds has not yet truly entered the mainstream, you might want to add an RSS explanation page that describes how to set up a feed reader and other relevant information.

▶ **Blogger Profiles**: Highlight your blog contributors by adding photos, relevant biographies, and contact information for each blogger.

▶ **Additional Content**: As you produce posts for your blog, you may develop content you would like to persist and not fall into the archives (e.g., help or instructional pages, key resources, updates).

▶ ENABLE EASE OF NAVIGATION

Consider the ways in which your readers will navigate your blog. Previous posts will cycle off the front of your blog as new content is posted on top. How will regular readers find content they once read and wish to see again? How will new readers explore past content? Ideally you will provide a few ways for them to locate previous posts.

Links to Previous Posts

On some blogs, once you scroll to the bottom of the front page, there will be a link to previous posts. I like this feature for new readers who just want to keep paging back over time to see your previous posts. Otherwise they may have to page through archives or read randomly through categories. I fear they may just not bother reading your previous content.

Archives

Whether you provide access to archived posts by chronological list or calendar format (see earlier section, "Sidebar Design"), it is important to make past posts available. This allows someone to comprehensively search past posts. It also gives a visual representation as to how long the blog has been operating. While this may seem insignificant now, when you are just starting out, seeing the months and years accumulate gives a sense of accomplishment to the bloggers and lends an air of authority to the blog itself.

Categories

The average person doesn't really care about finding previous content by date. They are more likely to be looking for information by subject. Give some thought to the subject areas you will be covering and create thematic categories for access to blog posts (see Figure 3.4). Categories are the equivalent to subject headings in the library catalog and should be a controlled vocabulary.

If your library or organization has a search engine that works with a taxonomy or metadata, take this into account when creating categories. You want your relevant individual blog posts to be pulled up when someone is searching the full Web site for a certain term. You can use terms that are already in the taxonomy, or, more likely, you can link up your categories with the relevant name in the taxonomy using some-

▶ Figure 3.4: Category List on the Turning the Page . . . Blog of the Public Library at Cincinnati and Hamilton County (www2.cincinnatilibrary.org/blog)

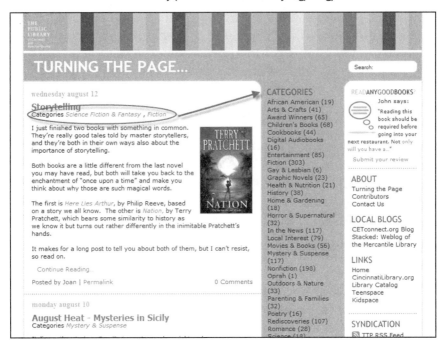

thing like a thesaurus or synonym ring. If you are lucky enough to have a taxonomy administrator in your organization, that person will be able to advise you on the best approach.

Once you have set up your categories, review them periodically for usefulness. If some are not being used, remove them. Perhaps there are some you should add. Again, keep in mind your organizational taxonomy if you are tying back to it.

It is a good idea to discuss categories with all your blog authors. Determine if they will be permitted to add categories or if there is a procedure for suggesting new categories. Consider allowing them to add tags as they want on an ad hoc basis (see "Effective Tagging Techniques" under "Develop Blog Content" for further discussion).

Author Posts

If you have a multiauthor blog, it is good practice to include a link to individual authors' posts so that you can see any one author's posts all together. You can make this as sophisticated as you like, but one simple way to accomplish this is to include author names as categories.

Popular Posts

Some bloggers like to list links to their most popular posts on the front of their blogs, often at the bottom of the page or in a sidebar. This showcases their best work and also helps extend the life of past blog posts. Ideally this is done automatically using the statistics of traffic to the blog. To locate an application that will do this for you, search your blog platform's Web site or search Google for "popular posts widget" or "popular posts plug-in." You will likely need to add a piece of code into your blog's HTML code to install.

Related Posts

Similar to popular posts, there are small applications for pulling up posts related to the blog post you have just written. The source for the related posts could be your own blog or others' blogs. Again, to locate an application for your blog platform, search for "related posts widget" or "related posts plug-in."

Permalinks

To direct someone to a specific blog post, have a URL that links directly to the post. This is more efficient than giving out the general blog Web address and then trying to describe how to find the post. The specific URL is called a "permalink." You may need to click through a blog post on the site to find the post's permalink. The permalink will usually link to the full blog post and comments. The UHD Library Blog from the University of Houston–Downtown Library (see Figure 3.5) has a link to the permalink for each post for the convenience of anyone wishing to cite their blog.

▶ DESIGN FOR USABILITY

Usability refers to the way visitors find their way around a Web site and whether they find the site accessible or not. Whole Web sites and books have been written on this subject, so we'll just look at some of the key areas.

Simplicity and Feature Choice

Err on the side of keeping the look of your blog simple. Too many features, widgets, and links can overwhelm your readers. When starting out, don't try to add every feature in at once. Start modestly and add

▶ Figure 3.5: Use of Permalinks on the UHD Library Blog from the University of Houston-Downtown Library (http://uhdlibrary.typepad.com)

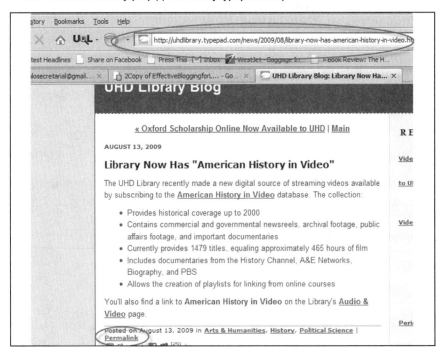

on as needed. Try out some features, and if your readers are not finding them helpful, remove them. Think about your overall strategy when adding features—do they support your main goals?

A lot of people find too many widgets (discussed later) in the sidebars to be annoying. Keep widgets to a minimum, and streamline the look of those you have as much as possible. This way, when you want something to really stand out in the sidebar—such as a button promoting a big library foundation fund-raising campaign—people will actually notice it.

Remember, too, that you don't need to implement everything you read about in this book. Pick and choose!

Accessibility

Accessibility is arguably the most important aspect of usability to consider. As with any Web site design, build your blog in such a way that it is usable by everyone, including those who have difficulty seeing, hearing, or making precise movements. Traditionally, accessibility features have been directed at making the Internet usable by those with hearing and vision disabilities, but they also benefit seniors, those with learning disabilities, and those with physical disabilities. In short, almost all of us can benefit from improved accessibility.

U.S. Federal Laws

All U.S. federal government Web sites must comply with the Section 508 Federal Accessibility Standards. The majority of these standards are addressed in the *Research-Based Web Design & Usability Guidelines* from the U.S. Department of Health and Human Services (www.usability.gov/pdfs/guidelines .html). This guide also references the Section 508 Web site (www .section508.gov) from the IT Accessibility and Workforce Division of the U.S. General Services Administration. These are excellent resources for all of us.

To familiarize yourself with specific accessibility issues, explore the W3C Web Accessibility Initiative (www.w3.org/WAI/intro/accessibility.php), which is in the continual process of developing guidelines and refining best practices. The "How to Make Your Blog Accessible" pages from All Access Blogging (www.allaccessblogging.com) provide a thorough discussion.

Also, I highly recommend having someone demonstrate for you a screen reader as used by blind Web site visitors. Or search YouTube for the phrase "screen reader" to locate some demos. This will give you an appreciation of some of the obstacles people can face when using what seems like a well-designed Web site. For improved accessibility, here are some simple practices you should implement from the beginning:

▶ Choose fonts and colors that people can read; dark text on a light background works best. Make sure the font is not too small.
▶ Make links distinct, when possible reserving bold and/or underlining only for links.
▶ Ensure that all visual elements include a text equivalent. Use the "alt" HTML code to describe each visual.
▶ For audio and video, include captions, transcripts, and/or descriptions.
▶ For Web links, use text that makes sense when read out of context. Avoid using "click here" links, because they won't make sense to someone tabbing through a list of links with a screen reader.
▶ Use headings, lists, and a consistent structure. Use CSS for layout wherever possible.
▶ For widgets and plug-ins, provide alternative content in case your active features are not accessible or unsupported by someone's browser.

- ▶ For tables, ensure that line-by-line reading makes sense. Summarize the table content.
- ▶ Try to go without CAPTCHA for preventing comment spam. CAPTCHA is a challenge (usually difficult to read text) that quizzes users to see if they are human or an automated bot on the Web spreading spam. If you must use CAPTCHA, use one with an audio challenge as an alternative to the visual challenge.
- ▶ Organize the elements in your sidebar with titles that are text rather than images. For any images in the sidebar, again make sure there is an alt code to it in the HTML.
- ▶ Break your blog posts into paragraphs.
- ▶ Use headings in your blog posts. Keep the headings meaningful and short so that people using readers can scan through the post quickly. Instead of using the bold feature to make the heading appear distinct, use your blog's heading tags if they are available. In the HTML code, headings will be between heading tags, such as:
  - ➤ <h1> and </h1> codes (first level headings),
  - ➤ <h2> and </h2> second level or subheading codes, and
  - ➤ <h3> and </h3> third level or sub-subheading codes.
- ▶ Use your blog software's feature for making lists rather than using asterisks or dashes. Someone using a screen reader who comes across a list will be told what is coming up, including how many items are in the list. If it is a list of links, this will also prevent the reader from running them all together.

This may sound like a lot at first, but it is much easier to put all of this in place when you are creating a Web site or blog rather than to fix it later. It will also seem easier once you get into the habit of doing things like adding alt codes in for visuals.

Finally, if you do have access to someone using a screen reader, it is a good idea to have that person check your site for accessibility and suggestions for improvements.

Navigation and Information Architecture

Information architecture has to do with how the pages of a Web site are organized, and navigation concerns how you get around or navigate the site. Keep in mind what we just learned about accessibility in the previous section as you work on the navigation and information architecture elements: the cleaner and better organized the page, the more everyone will benefit. In many ways the information architecture of a blog is predetermined: you have past posts on individual pages and also in a scroll, with most recent first and oldest last. You do want to create ways for people to find their way around, however. In particular, blogs are very good at showing the most recent few posts, but it can be a lot more difficult locating older posts.

It is a good idea to create your own guidelines for usability and accessibility, describing how links will be created, how multimedia elements such as graphics, photographs, audio, and video will be added, and explaining why you have chosen to structure the navigation as you have. This will be a useful resource for others working with the blog you are creating.

Link Titles

In your links to other Web sites or Web pages, include text that indicates what you are linking to. This is known as a "link title" or "title description." It is especially useful when linking from an image or other graphic, but, for accessibility, it should also be included when linking from text. Unfortunately, you cannot create this automatically with most blog platforms.

It is available as an option with WordPress's visual editor. When I create blog posts on Slaw.ca, WordPress allows me to type in the title to the blog post. The underlying HTML code for a title looks like this:

```
<a title="Canadian Press: Fraudster posing as a
friend stuck overseas without funds cons Good
Samaritans" href="http://www.google.com/hostednews
/canadianpress/article/ALeqM5ivW-V6PiO14-F_
6y6oeu2OAaafnw">Canadian Press story</a>
```

Figure 3.6 shows what this code translates into and looks like on the blog.

Persistent Navigation

Not everyone will enter your blog from the front page. If you are lucky, some of your blog posts will be highly ranked on Google and bring traffic in on their own. So, it is important to have all navigation features, including access to archives, category or tag lists, and search boxes, on all pages, including individual blog posts. Fortunately, existing blog software takes care of this for you. You will also want to have your brand or logo, and a link back to the front page, on all pages.

▶ Figure 3.6: Blog Post on the Slaw Blog (http://slaw.ca) Showing Link Title

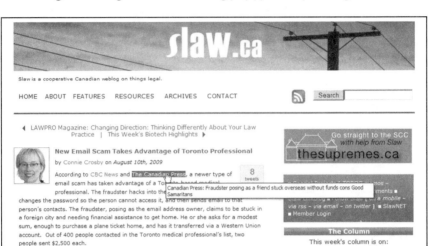

Preview Pop-Ups

Some blog platforms allow you to show a preview of a page you are linking to on another Web site. The reader runs the cursor over the link and the preview shows in a pop-up. Some people like this feature as it means they can have a quick look at a site without clicking on the link, while others find it annoying. Whether you use this feature or not will depend on your audience. If you do enable it, pay attention to any comments (for or against) that you receive. If you are in doubt whether to use it, it is probably best not to.

Opening New Browser Windows

When someone clicks on a link from the site, that site can either open in the same browser window, thus taking the reader off your Web site, or open in a separate browser window or tab. You can preset which you would like to take place, but individuals can also sometimes set this as a preference from their own browsers. Your blog software will likely have this preference as a setting. The HTML code that results usually adds the tag "target="_blank" to a link, for example:

```
<a href="http://www.librarian.net/"target="_blank
">Librarian.net</a>
```

Some prefer this feature because it means your readers do not actually leave your site. Others do not like it because it opens too many pages at once, and they prefer to use the "back" button instead. This often comes down to personal preference, so again pay attention to what your readers tell you.

Whichever you decide to do, be consistent with all your links. There is nothing more annoying than having most of your links open one way and then having one or two act in a different way. If you do decide to have links open on a separate page, do not use preview pop-ups.

Page Layout

Blogs typically have a main column where the blog posts appear. This column is usually wider than the sidebar columns, which can be on the right, left, or both. Because in the Western world we usually read left to right, use at most one sidebar on the left so you are not giving up prime browsing space to ephemeral features of the site. It is acceptable, however, to have two right sidebars. A more recent style is to have some of the features in a separate section or even a few columns on the bottom of the site (see Figure 3.7). In this case, show only one or two recent blog posts at a time so that your readers can actually find the features at the bottom.

▶ Figure 3.7: Three Columns at the Bottom of Steve Matthews' Web Strategy Blog (www .stemlegal.com/strategyblog) for Stem Legal

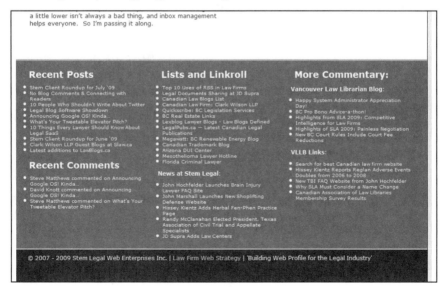

Illustrations and Graphics

Adding visuals to your blog posts can liven up the writing, illustrate points being made in the text, and provide a more enjoyable experience overall for most of your readers. Visuals include photographs, illustrations, and graphs or charts. Here are some pointers for using graphics:

- ▶ Be aware of the copyright status of other people's images, especially photographs and illustrations. Look for those that are made available under Creative Commons (http://creativecommons .org). You can search for photographs available under Creative Commons on Flickr's Web site using its advanced search feature (www.flickr.com/search/advanced). You may also purchase or use images from other sites. When in doubt, ask for permission.
- ▶ Better yet, try your hand at creating your own images—take photographs of interesting things, and learn how to use graphics software such as CorelDraw and Photoshop.
- ▶ You can also commission someone else to create illustrations and images for your site. Perhaps you have a colleague who is talented in this area who can be recruited to contribute.
- ▶ Remember those who will not be able to see your blog by ensuring that all visual elements include a text equivalent. Use the alt HTML code as shown earlier to describe each visual.
- ▶ Avoid using little animated graphics. Although they are used on many Web sites, they make the site look outdated and amateurish. If you do feel compelled to use them, use them very sparingly.

Advertising

Give careful thought about whether you will allow advertising on your blog. Some bloggers add Google Ads to their sites to generate some nominal income. Others take on paid ads or ads in exchange for favors in kind. Depending on the kind of organization you are in, you may or may not be at liberty to include ads on your site.

If you decide to include ads, decide what kind of ads are acceptable for your blog. Ads on your blog imply a type of endorsement, so include ads only for Web sites, products, or events that you want to be associated with and would recommend to others. It's a good idea to draw up some guidelines for acceptable or unacceptable ads and review them periodically. They'll come in handy when you are approached by third parties to post their ads.

International Users

Your blog will likely be read not only by your local community but also by others around the world. With the advent of general library Web sites, libraries now serve the global community. Many people around the world speak English, and online automated translation services such as Google Translate make access to blogs in other languages even easier. Keep this in mind in your writing—take real care not to write something offensive to those of other cultures. If you are writing about another culture, it might even be a good idea to consult with someone from that community to ensure you are not writing something inflammatory. Sometimes what appears innocuous to those in one culture is cause for concern in another. Here are some additional tips:

- ▶ Avoid too many idioms or slang. While these may mean something to you, someone else may not understand their meaning even if they have the same mother tongue.
- ▶ Cultural events and holidays vary from country to country. Not everyone celebrates Christmas, and even Thanksgiving falls on different dates in the United States and Canada (and is not celebrated at all outside North America). Also, sports-related phrases may not be universal. Not everyone knows about baseball or cricket.
- ▶ Words and spellings vary from country to country as well.

▶ ESTABLISH YOUR LIBRARY'S BRAND

Branding is not just your logo, but how you present your organization publicly and also your reputation with others. Keep in mind how you are presenting your blog on behalf of your library and how it will be best received by the readers you are targeting. Present the look of your blog as professionally as possible, and be consistent. Once you have settled on the following elements, use the same format everywhere.

Library Name

From blog title to individual blog posts and any related e-mail messages, use the same form of your library name. Changing it even slightly (from "City of Carla Library" to "Carla City Library") can be confusing to others.

Logo

Include a good, clean version of your library or organization's logo on all pages of the blog. If you are creating a logo from scratch, keep in mind how it looks both on the screen and in print. How will it look on letterhead or blown up on a sign? Also think about what colors it will contain, and how it will look if printed in black and white.

Colors

Use colors for the various elements of your blog, including the blog post text, links, sidebar text, titles, header, blog post background, and sidebar backgrounds. Learn what the numeric values for these are so you can be precise in your coding and graphic creation. Make note of both RGB and hexadecimal ("hex") values where possible.

Fonts

Pick one or two fonts and stick with them. Mixing too many fonts will make the site look too "busy." Decide how headings will be formatted. Keep in mind font size, especially when considering accessibility for seniors and those with visual impairment.

Do as many large corporations do, and create a style guide for your blog that records all the particulars of your branding. This will help anyone developing new content to maintain a consistent look.

▶ DEVELOP BLOG CONTENT

23 Things to Do with Your Blog Posts

Coming up with content for your blog is fun at first but, over time, may become more challenging. Here are some types of posts you may consider for your blog—can you think of others?

1. **Breaking News**: Blogs allow for pulling together late-breaking industry or current events news quicker than most other communication vehicles. Pay attention to sources such as Google News, newswire services, and BreakingNews (BNO news) on Twitter (http://twitter.com/BreakingNews) to find breaking news.

2. **Library and Community News and Events**: Posting news from the library is an obvious use for blogs. Readers will not go to your blog for this purpose alone, however, so you have to give them juicier content to keep them coming back. If you are writing for a particular group or community, one way to do this is to write about community news and events as well.

3. **Opinion**: Librarians tend to shy away from controversy in an attempt to not offend and to remain neutral. And yet, readers like to see passion, and a bit of controversy does well to attract atten-

tion and comments to blogs. Take a risk periodically and write an opinion piece!

4. **Resource/Link List**: Pick a subject that is hot with your readership, or even just one that they find interesting, and build a list of Web resources for them. This will bring readers to your blog, give them new resources to explore, and, if you develop a number of these resource lists over time, make your blog a must-read site for researchers.

5. **Ideas/Inspirational Storytelling**: There is something poetic about the writing on the Berkeley Heights Public Library Book Blog. The blog post "The Six Bean Story: or why gardening can drive you crazy," by Anne about her garden and Mother Goose, is inspired (http://bhplnjbookgroup.blogspot.com/2009/06/six-bean-story-or-why-gardening-can.html). We need to hear more personal voices like this in our blogging.

6. **Aggregate List/Guide**: Similar to #4, Resource/Link List, why not build a list of resources available in your library on a subject of interest? If possible, link into the individual item records in your OPAC so readers can get more information, including location and keywords. This will show people the power of your OPAC and help make it a focal point as a research tool.

7. **New Acquisitions**: This is another obvious use for a library blog—why not point out the best of new materials coming into your library? Focus on items that are topical but might go unnoticed otherwise. If you produce newsletters to communicate new titles, can you re-purpose them for the blog? Can you do away with a paper newsletter altogether? The answers will depend on the culture of your library users. You may need to show them the blog posts and ask their preference.

8. **Book Discussion**: Beyond new acquisitions, feature existing books in the collection, again linking readers into the OPAC record for additional location information.

9. **Book Recommendations**: If you have a reader advisory service, why not have a blog to highlight it? Base the blog posts on popular types of books or subjects your library gets asked about frequently. Use this as a way to increase borrowing of lesser-known titles.

10. **Review/Analysis**: One of our roles as librarians is to review sources, guide our clients to the best sources, and help them learn how to critically evaluate the sources themselves. Blogs are excellent tools for this type of discussion. Keep your reviews balanced and factual, especially if they contain negative judgments and are publicly posted, because the companies that make the products can be very sensitive to public criticism.

11. **Humorous**: Seemingly at the other end of the spectrum of blog posts are those that are humorous. Quite often, however, humor

is used to couch criticism on blogs. For example, the Awful Library Books blog (http://awfullibrarybooks.wordpress.com) discusses "awful" books found in libraries, describes them in an amusing manner, and explains why they should be weeded from library collections. While the intention is to amuse, the blog does get the point across that libraries are not archives to indefinitely hold all materials they have ever owned.

12. **How-To/Tutorial**: Libraries produce numerous checklists and "how-to" content to supplement more formal training. Blogs are good places to post some or all of this content online. Consider using multimedia formats such as graphics, video, and screencasts in creative ways to liven up otherwise flat content.

13. **Suggestion Board**: Many large libraries have suggestion boards. Why not post responses to suggestions onto the blog as well? You could even build a Web form to get more suggestions.

14. **Interview**: This may possibly be my favorite type of blog post! I like meeting new people, interviewing them, and relating the core of what they are saying to readers. Ideally I like to do this in an audio (podcast) format, but it can be done in writing as well. If you conduct an interview via e-mail or another written format, do as journalists do and make note of that for your readers because it can affect the tone and responses you get during questioning.

15. **Case Study**: Along the same lines as #10, Review/Analysis, this is a more in-depth type of post that looks at a real-life example in a subject area and examines and describes it so that others may learn from the example. Vicky Owens, in her blog Vicki Owens' Topically Technological Library Blog, includes case studies as part of her research project for the Liverpool John Moores University, including these on mobile learning:
    a. Case Study 1: West Cheshire College (February 24, 2009): http://vickiowensm-learningblog.blogspot.com/2009/02/case-study-1-west-cheshire-college-wcc.html
    b. Case Study 2: London School of Economics (March 5, 2009): http://vickiowensm-learningblog.blogspot.com/2009/03/case-study-2-london-school-of-economics.html
    c. Case Study 3: Tate Modern (March 6, 2009): http://vickiowensm-learningblog.blogspot.com/2009/03/case-study-3-tate-modern.html

16. **Snarky or Contrarian**: Similar to #11, Humorous, this type of blog post is meant to provoke and may not be funny to all. It is meant to be controversial and inspire people to comment. Tread carefully with this type of blog post, as it takes superior writing skill to pull it off. Warm up by reading some of the great satirists to see how they did it. If you are writing just a one-time blog post on an otherwise serious blog, your readers may misinterpret the tone as

serious. I suggest somehow indicating these as editorials or opinion pieces if you feel compelled to try your hand at this style.

17. **Diary Entry**: While you always want to remain professional when representing your organization, you do need to make your writing engaging and readable. Periodically telling personal stories, provided that they tie back to the blog's purpose and theme, can work well.

18. **Video**: Whether you carefully select videos from sources such as YouTube, CommonCraft, or TED, or produce your own, videos on blogs capture people's attention. Be sure to include some text with the video to improve accessibility for some of your audience and to help search engines find and index the blog post more easily.

19. **Images**: Some blogs are dedicated just to images and are known as "photoblogs." You can include photos and other types of images in your blog posts as a way to present content in a refreshing manner and provide information in another format. Read the earlier section "Illustration and Graphics" under "Design for Usability" for advice before you get started.

20. **Podcast Episode Summary**: A podcast is an audio show made available through the Internet, such as through Apple's iTunes or the podcast's Web site. Because podcasts are by nature a serial and therefore syndicated with RSS, a blog is a perfect place to store and distribute episodes. In addition to the audio file, it is a good idea to post a summary of your episode in text so that, as with #18, Video, accessibility is improved and the show can be better indexed by search engines.

21. **Charts and Graphs**: Make your content interesting with images other than photographs, such as charts and graphs. These can help represent some of the information you want to present and give some talking points for your blog post. As with other types of images, ensure you have the right to post the charts and graphs. You can also create your own.

22. **Surveys**: The Chattanooga State Augusta R. Kolwyck Library is a champion at running quick polls from its blog to find out what people are thinking. While these are more "straw polls" than legitimate surveys, they can get quick insight into the library clientele's thinking while at the same time communicate the library's thinking process. See, for example, "Question: Should the library have a Facebook page?—Three quick questions" (http://library.chattanoogastate.edu/blog/?p=323) or "Want Graphic Novels? Take Our Quick Survey" (http://library.chattanoogastate.edu/blog/?p=193).

23. **Scholarly Articles**: Open access to scholarly writing is slowly gaining popularity among academics. They are looking at a number

of different vehicles for making articles available and yet still allow publishers to charge for published versions of those articles. Some professors and researchers self-publish their articles on their blogs, and the reader needs to keep in mind that these have not gone through the editing and peer review process. Self-publishing can, however, give others faster access to their research and theories and get faster feedback. And, if peers are willing to post constructive criticisms in the comments, this can be a sort of peer review tool. Libraries can possibly facilitate this process by making articles available from their blogs.

What to Post

Do your library colleagues proud and really leverage your research skills to pull together some truly killer content.

Communicate to Your Audience/Community

Keep your audience in mind at all times. If your blog is for children, don't address the writing to parents. If your audience is a professional one, be personable but not too casual. Go ahead and include those news and notice type items, but ensure you inject a healthy dose of personality. People are visiting your blog voluntarily, and you want to ensure they come back! Think about what your audience is interested in, and write to those interests. Ideally you want to use the blog to join with and hopefully become part of the community you are serving. Blogging is just one method of accomplishing this and should be part of your larger public relations strategy.

Answer Questions Received by the Library

If you get asked the same question by a number of people, it may be an appropriate topic of discussion on your blog. Take care about privacy and confidentiality—don't identify people unless you have their permission, and don't quote their original question in case it can identify them. Of course, if you are responding to questions posted in the comments of your blog, then you are well served to refer to that person's question when responding. The difference is that that person has shared the question publicly and is expecting a public response.

Look at Your Web Traffic Statistics

What are people searching for when on your Web site? You can find this in your site statistics. Is there content available on these topics? You may want to develop something that answers this need. If your blog is pulling in traffic for a certain topic that fits well with your mandate, add more blog posts expanding on the topic, making your blog a real "go-to" resource for the subject matter. This is one way to leverage a potential existing audience and keep readers coming back to your site without ever having to ask them what they would like to see.

Get Inspiration from Other Sources

RSS feeds and Google Alerts are the "secret weapon" of some of the top bloggers. Use your research skills and really dig out some of those sources that may be hidden from the average researcher's eyes. Don't forget paid subscription services such as Factiva and Medline that provide RSS feeds for their searches.

Consider using Web site tracking tools such as InfoMinder (www .infominder.com) and WebSite Watcher (http://aignes.com), which tell you when a Web site has been updated. Sabrina Pacifici keeps a current list of these tools on her Web site LLRX.com (www.llrx.com/features/ciguide.htm#onlinetools). Use everything you have at your disposal to make your blog content great.

Ask Your Readers a Question

Is there a burning question on your mind? A recent controversy you have come across? Asking questions is a powerful way to get some comments. Ask your readers for their opinions, their advice, and their stories. This works particularly well if you already have a few people commenting on your blog. You might seed some answers by asking other staff members or friends for their comments. If you do this often enough you can get the ball rolling with some good audience participation and help engage those people more with what you are writing on the blog.

Ideas for Those Days When You Have No Ideas

Keep a "rainy day" file of potential blog topics. These are topics that are not urgent and can be published at any time. Failing that, here are other ways to generate blog ideas:

1. Surf key Web sites on a topic to see if they have any news.
2. Search Google for some key topics.
3. Check the latest news stories in Google News.
4. Watch the 24-hour news channels for that obscure topic everyone else might miss.
5. Ask followers on Twitter or Facebook what they would like to read about.
6. Think about upcoming events you are excited about attending.

7. Look at things you are writing for other purposes; is there something there that can be shared?

Social media/PR maven Chris Brogan has a blog post at www .chrisbrogan.com titled "20 Blog Topics to Get You Unstuck" (March 17, 2009) that has even more ideas to inspire you. He is a master of blogging consistently, frequently more than once a day. Be sure to have a good look around his blog for additional ideas while you are there.

When to Post

Timing Is Everything

You write that brilliant blog post and wait. And wait. And you wonder how can there be no reaction? And yet, three months later it suddenly becomes one of your most popular posts of all time. Why is this? There could be two different things at play: one is that your regular readers have not found it necessarily of interest, but it rises to the top in search engines for other people who are interested in the topic. The other thing is timing. Something may have happened that suddenly makes your post relevant.

Also keep in mind that some topics have shorter "half-lives" than others. If there is a hot topic that comes out in current events today, and if you can push out a post on a topic immediately—hopefully today—you may get an audience for a post that you would not get for the same post a week from now.

Drafting Posts in Advance

One of the secrets of the great bloggers is drafting posts in advance. You can develop a whole coherent series of blog posts, write them all at once when you are inspired, and gradually release them over time. Another trick some successful bloggers use is to have a large number of blog posts on various topics in progress. As they find new content on a topic, they add it to the draft post. Once the content seems complete, they do a final edit and release it to the world.

Releasing Timed Posts

Some blog software will allow you to automatically publish posts at designated times on specific days. This way you can plan in advance for absences such as vacations—it can appear as though you were never away! It is also ideal for any content that is time sensitive, such as press releases.

Writing Tips for Bloggers

Length of Posts

Posts can vary from short, one- or two-line entries to longer, more formal articles. The key is your audience. What kind of attention span will they have? Are they looking for quick hits of information or detailed analyses? What age or reading level are they?

Just as it is a good idea to vary content, it is also a good idea to vary the length of your posts. If your audience would not be interested in long tracts of text, incorporate a series of visuals such as photographs or other graphics to tell a story.

Tips on Formatting

Writing for the Web is very different from writing business reports or other professional hard copy documents. To maximize readability of your blog posts, write succinctly. Think about the language you are using; how can you liven up the tone? Add headings to break up the text and allow people to easily skim and find what they want to read. Use heading formatting codes rather than just using bold for headings so that those using screen readers can quickly scan the sections. Use other tricks like bulleted lists to make your posts even easier to scan and visuals such as photographs to catch the eye and make the post more visually appealing.

Blog Post Titles

It is fun to come up with a clever title for your blog posts, but this may hinder people seeking your information via a search engine. Don't be too oblique with your titles! If you are writing about an event, mention the name of the event. If you are featuring a person, mention the person's name. Use words that describe your post or include key words that you hope the search engines find. You can even take this a step further by seeing how the words you are thinking of pull up in Google before using them. One way I combine the practical, traffic-drawing titles with the clever and fun is to use a main title and subtitle, making one practical and the other clever, for example:

- ▶ Dogs, Dogs, Dogs! Your Guide to Dog Breeds, Breeders, Training, and Kennels
- ▶ Zelda Fitzgerald: Living in the Shadow of F. Scott Fitzgerald
- ▶ Houston, We Have a Problem: Relationship Problems and How to Resolve Them

Linking Etiquette

Linking to other Web sites, blogs, etc., gives your readers additional resources if they have questions about a specific topic, and it makes it easy for them to locate a Web site you have mentioned. It gives credit to others and also helps with their search engine ranking. Here are a few tips about linking:

- ▶ You don't need permission to link.
- ▶ Add a title to the link for accessibility.
- ▶ Again for accessibility, don't take the text out of context, i.e., don't link to "Click here."
- ▶ Incorporate as many links to as much other relevant content as you can in your blog post.
- ▶ Do not link to unrelated content on the Internet; this is frowned upon as a "spammy" practice.

If your blog becomes popular, you may be invited by others to exchange links. Reciprocal linking at your discretion with other known organizations is fine, but beware there are a lot of people contacting owners of popular sites trying to get links. You are best to forego these as you do not want to build lists of links that are meaningless to your readers. This is another spammy practice to avoid.

Effective Tagging Techniques

Tags are labels that you can apply to individual posts (see Figure 3.8). Tags are informal and unstructured compared with categories, which are formal and structured. We label things in an ad hoc manner with tags, and different people will likely label things differently. While categories can give some hierarchical structure (as in a taxonomy), tags provide us with a more granular way to identify and locate posts of interest.

Usually categories are used for navigation to older posts on the blog site itself, whereas tags are used for outside search tools to find your blog posts. You do not need to list tags in your sidebar, although some like to post a tag cloud (a graphical representation of the most popular tags).

Not all blog platforms have tagging capability, so plug-ins can be used. Search Google for "tagging plug-in" or "tag plug-in," or search your platform's help forum or plug-in directory for "tag" or "tagging" to find the latest. WordPress, for example, has a Plug-in Directory; members of the WordPress community rate the plug-ins with a star sys-

▶ Figure 3.8: Individual Posts Tagged by the Authors on The Caird Library Blog from the National Maritime Museum in Greenwich (www.nmm.ac.uk/library)

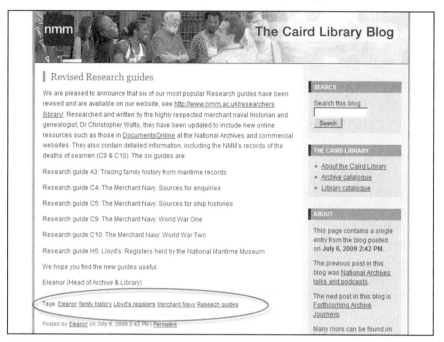

tem so you can determine which work best. Blogger does have tagging capability, although at times it is cumbersome.

It is a lot of work to apply tags retroactively, especially to older blogs. It is akin to going back and adding new subject headings to all of your library catalog records. Start tagging at the beginning, or close to the beginning, when you can easily tag new content as it is created.

Copyrighting Your Work

While we should assume that all worked posted to the Internet is copyrighted and would seek permission to use as appropriate, for clarity it is a good idea to specify the copyright on our own sites and content. Give some thought to your overall policy: do you want to reserve all rights so that others only use either with permission or according to fair use as provided by legislation? Would you like to remove all copyright and make your content completely open for others' use? Or perhaps you are in an agency that cannot copyright its works or that already has a copyright policy? Consider the culture of your readership. Is it common for them to share content?

Most bloggers fall somewhere in between: we want to take part in the big, collaborative community of the Internet and have our content generally open for use, but we don't want someone to take advantage of that and make money from our content or abuse the privilege. Creative Commons licensing was created for just this purpose.

Creative Commons is a nonprofit organization created to give individuals and organizations a standard way to give permission to use their works. The main Creative Commons Web site is http:// creativecommons.org, although you may have a different Web site specific to your country. You are best to follow the licensing for your country, even if your blog has an international audience. Creative Commons has several levels of restrictions, so decide which type of license you want. You can specify that your content can be reused by anyone or just for noncommercial reasons. You can request attribution and also designate whether someone is permitted to alter your content or not. Do you want to allow someone to build upon or "remix" what you have created into another creation? Creative Commons licenses and icons are available from http://creativecommons .org/about/licenses.

Whichever way you go, do add a copyright notice to your Web site either in the footer or (preferably) in a sidebar where people are more likely to see it. It can be as simple as using the copyright symbol ©, the name of your organization, and the date and updating the year every year.

Backing Up Content

While hopefully your host server will be reliable and not lose any of your content, it is a good idea to back it up on a regular basis. You never know when something might accidentally go wrong or when something you do might delete everything. This doesn't happen very often, but better safe than sorry.

Check whether your blog service includes backups. (Blogger, for example, does not, but it does tell you how to do it in its help files.) If it does, check whether this includes all content, including images and other multimedia you have loaded, or just the text. Some items, such as YouTube videos, are merely linked back to the originating site so you don't have to worry about those—just what you have uploaded to the blog server.

In addition to all of the database records (blog posts), also back up your blog template periodically. How often do you back up content for your organization? Where does the blog fit in as far as priority intellectual capital for your organization? Decide whether it is high priority (backed up every day) or regular priority (likely backed up once a week).

Also back up the content when you are making any changes to the site, such as upgrading to a new version of the blog platform. If you are changing the template in any way, be sure to back up your existing template so you can revert back if necessary.

If you are hosting the blog yourself on your own servers, ensure that IT staff are including it in their regular backups. Find out how it is backed up and where the backed-up files are stored. Are they stored onsite or off site? If you are responsible for backing up the site, consult with your IT department on setting up the process. It can be complicated and varies depending on the software you are using and the underlying database (SQL, MySQL, or other). Once you establish a method, it should be relatively easy to do. Maintain a regular schedule for backing up (daily, every second day, once a week), and designate someone to back it up, as well as an alternative person in case this person is away.

▶ LAUNCH YOUR BLOG

You are joining the blogosphere, so what better way to kick things off than to let other bloggers know you are joining their ranks? You can of course tell every blogger you know in a "scatter gun" method of marketing (e-mail to everyone!). To avoid such impersonal, spam-like press releases, be selective and reach out to a few bloggers personally.

Determine Who the Influencers Are

What market are you trying to reach? Find the key bloggers (or "influencers") in this sector. Sometimes easier said than done! Use your research skills to find those who seem to pull up well in Google searches and seem to be quoted on other blogs. Then do two things with your list of potentials—see how popular they are (check external links) and then contact the ones you think will be good influencers.

Check External Links

To determine how popular a blog site is, check its external links. Do this by searching Google for "links:DOMAIN URL." For example, let's say you are looking to launch a blog appealing to science fiction readers, and you have identified the blog SFSignal (http://sfsignal.com) as a possible influencer you want to reach. Search Google for links :http://sfsignal.com (with no spaces) to see how many links are coming in to SFSignal. The results of this search are shown in Figure 3.9.

On the day I searched this, I found over 2,400 links to the blog. Pretty good for a blog! You will want to compare this with the other blogs on your list and decide if they are priority blogs or not.

Contact Blog Owners

Next contact the blog owners directly to let them know about your new blog (remember that just forwarding a press release will likely be seen as spam and get deleted). It is a good idea to contact these people in advance and build a bit of a rapport. Perhaps you can ask them for advice on writing to your specific audience before you actually launch the blog? Approach them in a professional but personable way. If you can build up a friendship with the person, you are more likely to be well-received when you ask for help spreading the news about your new blog.

Announce on all Social Network Sites

Think about how you are going to announce the blog to the world. If some members of your library staff are participating in social networks, either on behalf of the library or individually, involve them to

▶ Figure 3.9: Google Search Results for Search of Links Pointing to the SFSignal Blog (http://sfsignal.com)

get the word out as much as possible. I will talk about Facebook and Twitter specifically, but there are many other social networks around. Think about where your audience is, and go to the audience. It helps to have built a rapport or friendships with them in advance.

Facebook. There are several approaches you can take to spread the word via Facebook. Pick those that work for you and your organization:

- ▶ Simple word of mouth: add a link to your new blog from library staff's personal Facebook profiles, and e-mail your friends with the link.
- ▶ If your library has a page or a group, add a link. Make an announcement under "Recent News," and send an e-mail to all members.
- ▶ Find related Facebook groups, join them, and add a link or a note to the wall mentioning the new blog. Take care how you word this. You do not want to alienate a potential fan base with an announcement that is perceived as commercial advertising. This method is most successful if you become a member of the group in advance, get to know the culture of the group, and participate.
- ▶ Add your blog to Facebook's NetworkedBlogs app, and then ask your friends or members of your page or group to join.
- ▶ Create a Facebook page for your blog, and invite others to become a fan.
- ▶ Create a widget with Widgetbox for your new blog and place it onto your Facebook page and profile. You can even hand out your widgets to others to post on their Facebook pages (this is discussed in more detail later in "Blog Widgets and Other Tools").
- ▶ Advertising: don't discount it! Put a community-friendly graphic together, and decide how targeted an audience you want and how long you want the ad to run. Facebook has the power of delivering your message to a highly selective audience. You can choose the specific audience by location and gender. You can pay by number of clicks through on your ad or by how many impressions are delivered. You can set a daily budget. Watch the demographics on who is clicking through on your ad, and adjust your ad to hopefully improve uptake by your target audience. Remember, people are far more likely to click on Facebook advertising if it is from a local, familiar face than from some of the nameless corporations we see advertising.

The Freeport Public Library created a page on Facebook for fans of its Freeport Public Library Teen Book Blog (see Figure 3.10). The library invited teens to sign up and post a book review to the wall in ex-

▶ Figure 3.10: The Freeport Public Library Teen Book Blog on Facebook

change for a prize. Once they get 100 or more members signed up, they can then claim a unique URL from Facebook that will be easier to refer people to than the cumbersome URL http://www.facebook.com/group.php?gid=130109800960.

Remember, before you make a huge effort of jumping to Facebook, think about whether your audience resides there. If it is a business blog, is your business audience on Facebook? If it is a blog for children, are they there?

Twitter. If you have an existing Twitter account for the library or if any staff members have personal accounts, again push out a brief note once or twice about the new blog. Once you have the blog up and running, push out links to your best posts. Don't mention all posts, or people will find you too self-promotional. It is also important to have other content on your Twitter stream so that people will connect with you personally. If you are pointing them to the best of the Web regardless of whether it is from your blog or not, they are more likely to read the links you provide from your blog.

Seed the Blog with Whiz-Bang Content

Once people come to your site, you want them to like what they see and come back. Make sure you have some good content before you open it up to everyone. Practice your best blogging skills and spend the time putting together content with lively writing and with images (photos or graphics) to make it really eye-catching. Featuring people is a great way to go (such as with profiles or interviews) to give your blog a personal feel right from the beginning. Really show your passion for the topic—don't be afraid to "geek out"!

Join a Blog Carnival

To get some eyes looking at your blog, consider participating in a blog carnival. A blog carnival is a very special type of blog post. It summarizes the previous week's (or two weeks') worth of best blog posts on the Internet on a specific subject or theme. What makes it carnival-like is that it moves around from blog to blog. To find a blog carnival on your subject, check the Blog Carnival Web site (http://blogcarnival .com/bc). Additional carnivals may be found by Googling "blog carnival" and a subject.

Blog carnivals often have a Web page used to communicate with participants and readers, coordinate the schedule, and keep track of past and future posts. There are two ways for you to participate: submit blog posts for consideration in an upcoming carnival or host the carnival for a week. Start by suggesting some blog posts. Many bloggers use this opportunity to submit their own blog posts that they feel are particularly good or important and deserve more attention. You can do the same to promote your blog.

I have personally hosted two carnivals: the Blawg Review (carnival of law blogs; http://blawgreview.blogspot.com) and Carnival of the Infosciences (for library bloggers, now sadly defunct but still available at http://infosciences.pbworks.com). I found them to be a lot of work, so pick the date you register for wisely. Each carnival has its own rules and customs, so it is a good idea to read through some of the previous carnival posts before signing up and ideally participate with submissions first.

▶ ENCOURAGE PARTICIPATION IN YOUR BLOG

Getting things going with a blog is the hardest part. You write your first brilliant post and then wonder where the comments are. The truth is, you will need to build up a small catalog of good content before you really get noticed. If you are blogging once a day, this could happen quickly. If you are blogging once a week, it could be months before you start to build any readership. Throw some good efforts in at the beginning, and it will pay off as word of mouth spreads about your blog.

Strategies for Encouraging Comments

Depending on your audience, getting people to comment on your blog can be the most difficult part. Remember what we learned earlier from *Groundswell* in Chapter 1: many people are "Spectators" or "Joiners," but few are "Critics" willing to comment. And, depending on the audience you are appealing to, there may be more critics or fewer critics in the group than the average audience. I learned this with my own blog (http://conniecrosby.blogspot.com), which I have been writing for years. I have a large librarian following, and I know that people are reading because they tell me when I see them in person. And yet very few comments ever get posted to my blog. This is because librarians (or, at least, the ones reading my blog) are more likely to fall into the "Collectors," "Joiners," or "Spectators" demographic.

Tips on Encouraging Comments

▶ **Don't Put Obstacles in the Way**: Take care not to impede people from commenting. If you require them to register before commenting, they will not do it. Ideally comments should be free to add without any additional steps. To prevent spam, you may want to use a CAPTCHA feature, but take care because not all of these are accessible to people with Web readers. It is best not to have a CAPTCHA on, but people are generally used to it now.

▶ **Ask Questions to Get the Discussion Going**: One method of getting people commenting is to ask them questions or for feedback directly. Then, after posting, send the question out to your followers on Twitter, Facebook, and elsewhere inviting them to add their take. This tends to work if you have a following elsewhere.

▶ **Get Others to Help**: Don't let your blog suffer from the "empty dance floor" syndrome! A blog without comments is not going to attract commenters. Invite your fellow staff, friends, and colleagues to post their comments to get a discussion going. It might take several tries, but at some point you will notice one or two people you don't recognize chiming in.

▶ **Be Responsive**: Nothing is more discouraging to a commenter than to post a brilliant message and not get a response back. Be responsive and reply to your commenters in the comments. If you can't think of anything specific to say, at least thank them for contributing. This will encourage them to return.

Events

Hold an event on your blog. Make up a theme day, or tie into an event in your library. There are a lot of blog-based events happening on the

Internet as well, so consider joining one of them. Note who is sponsoring the event, as these can often be political or otherwise support a viewpoint that could alienate some members of your audience. Here are a few to get you started:

- ▶ Ada Lovelace Day (in March), http://findingada.com/blog/category/ada-lovelace-day: Bloggers post about women in technology who they admire.
- ▶ BlogDay (in August), http://www.blogday.org: A day of blog discovery—bloggers find and recommend five new (to them) blogs.
- ▶ Blog Action Day (in October), http://blogactionday.org: Bloggers promote charities and giving to help reduce poverty.

Guest Bloggers

Having a guest blogger can do a few nice things for your blog. A high-profile guest will bring some traffic to your site. Also, if the guest has a blog, he or she will likely promote the guest post, bringing some traffic as well. A guest blogger can also help supplement your content, so it is good to bring in a guest at times when your blog might be a little understaffed, such as during holidays.

Give your guest an idea of what you would like to see but leave the subject matter fairly open. Also give a timeline—when would you like the post(s) to go up? How many posts would you like to see? Set the parameters early for best success.

On the administrative side, you will need to figure out how the guest will post to the blog. Can you arrange for a guest password, do you need to set up a permanent new password, or will you be reposting on the guest's behalf?

If your guest is going to put a series of posts together, consider branding them with a series name and even a little graphic so they are easily identifiable. If you give all the posts a specific category or tag, you can link to them as a group from the sidebar of the blog.

Blog Posts from Reader Comments

When you start the ball rolling with some comments, you might find some inspiration there for a new blog post. Why not take it a step further and invite comments specifically so you can address them on the blog? This will hopefully get your existing audience interested and returning to see how you have responded. Perhaps they will even tell their family and friends about it.

▶ DEAL WITH NEGATIVE FEEDBACK

It is a mistake to close down negative conversations. You need these to validate the positive discussions. If everything is always positive, some of your potential audience may infer you are only presenting a one-sided viewpoint to benefit your organization.

The key is to ensure someone is monitoring the comments. Designate someone to cover this and to alert the blog contributors of anything they need to respond to.

Turn the Negative into Positive

Many times people are negative because they are passionate about the subject at hand and want to see their concerns addressed. The best way to work with negative comments is to thank the person and address the concerns. If you have to look into something and get back with a response later, say so—don't let the question hang for days without some sort of acknowledgment until you find the answer. Always be professional, not belittling, snarky, or angry. Anything you say that might look mean or retaliatory will reflect poorly on you and your organization.

Your responsiveness should reflect well on you. Quite often just responding, thanking the commenter, and addressing his or her concerns is enough to make that person a fan of your organization. Follow up—make sure that person is happy.

Keep this person in mind in the future. If you are looking for feedback on a service, perhaps this would be someone ideal to give you some constructive criticism.

Decide When to Keep and When to Remove Comments

Your blog comment policy comes in handy when unsavory comments are posted, and you are not quite sure what to do. Refer to your policy and see how the comment fits in, and how you said you would address it. Again, if it is just a negative comment, you are better to address it than remove it.

If the comment promotes hatred against a certain group or uses indecent language according to the norm of the audience you are writing for, you are likely within your right to remove the post. If possible, add a comment saying you have removed the post and why.

If you are unsure what to do, best to consult with coworkers and make a group decision. Think about adjusting your policy so that it covers future incidents.

Handle Trolls

Ah, trolls. They have been around since before the Internet began. These are commenters purposely being negative and contrary to get a reaction from others. They will argue and argue and try to keep the discussion going as long as they can. They are seeking attention and will likely keep coming back once they have found you. They have even been known to create another persona (known as "sock-puppets") sympathetic to the blog audience, and argue back and forth, trying to draw others in.

"Don't feed the trolls" is a saying those of us who have been on the Internet a long time use. Because they are seeking attention, the best way to get rid of trolls is to ignore them. They will hopefully get bored and leave. You may want to quietly ask others behind the scenes not to respond as well.

Unfortunately we often do not recognize trolls until we have engaged in some significant conversation and become frustrated with them. If you are plagued with trolls you will hopefully learn to recognize them over time.

Because trolls feed on anonymity, one way to reduce trolls is to force people to identify themselves with a name and an e-mail address before they can leave a comment. Of course, people can type anything in, so this is not foolproof.

Understand That Not Everyone Is a Blogger or Reads Blogs

Keep in mind that you may get negative comments about the existence of the blog itself from others in person or by e-mail. Not everybody understands what blogs can do, and some people view them negatively. Don't force reading of the blog on anyone.

Also realize that not all of your coworkers will be interested in blogging. Don't force someone to participate who is not interested, as this will not lead to success. You may find the person comes around later after seeing the interest the blog garners.

▶ GAIN A READERSHIP (AND KEEP IT!)

It is content that will capture your readers' attention. Without content, the following suggestions will bring people in temporarily, but they won't stick around for long.

Feed Reader Subscribers

While your blog comes with its own RSS feed, it is a good idea to feed this through a service that will monitor how many feed subscribers you have. Google's FeedBurner (http://feedburner.google.com) will do this for you. Copy your existing feed URL, paste it into the "burn a feed" box on the first page, and you will receive another RSS feed URL from FeedBurner. Use this new URL to post (along with the RSS icon) onto your blog instead of the RSS feed that came with your blog so you can see how many people subscribe to your feed.

To gain feed subscribers in the first place, be sure to have your feed prominently posted on the blog. Toward the top of one of your sidebars with the standard orange icon is ideal.

When you publicize the new blog in your newsletter or elsewhere, don't forget to mention the availability of the feed. Be prepared in case some of your readers ask for help in setting a reader up just to see your feed!

Link Love

Be kind with your links. When you mention someone or another organization, it is good to link to their Web site or blog. This helps boost them in the Google search rankings, thus giving the name of this little technique "link love." If they are monitoring the Web for mentions, they will see you have posted and hopefully either comment on your blog or respond on their own site. If you want someone specific to link to you, you might try writing a nice post about him or her.

Link Thanks

Conversely, keep an eye out for those who have linked back to you. You might want to reciprocate with a comment on their blog or thanks in your own blog, depending on the value of what the other person posted.

Blog Widgets and Other Tools

Widgets are little applications that can be attached to your blog (or other Web site) to do something very specific. They can do things like show the weather in your town, run a poll, or count how many visitors have been on your site. Some will go into your sidebar, some will add to the features of all your individual blog posts, and still others are ways to post content into individual blog posts.

There are literally thousands and thousands available from all sorts of sources; Google for the word "widgets" and you will see what I mean. Have a look also at Google Gadgets For Your Webpage (www.google .com/ig/directory?synd=open) and Yahoo! Widgets (http://widgets .yahoo.com). Some of these are for Web sites (including blogs), while others are meant for personal use on the desktop, so pay attention to this when you are selecting your widgets. Also keep your eyes open for widgets and features you like on other blogs for ideas. Just think what fun a Harry Potter and the Goblet of Fire Countdown would have been on your youth blog if it was around at the time.

Of course, you want to keep in mind the look and feel of your blog as well. Some widgets will let you adjust the color of the frames and resize them before you post. And for every visual element you add, make sure there is text code for anyone with the images turned off on their browsers, including those using Internet readers.

Posting a Widget to a Blog Post

Many video sharing and other sites provide you with code to easily repost the content to your blog site. YouTube (www.youtube.com) comes to mind. You can repost a video from YouTube into a blog post by using the embed code (HTML code) from the YouTube video page (see Figure 3.11).

▷ Figure 3.11: YouTube Embed Code

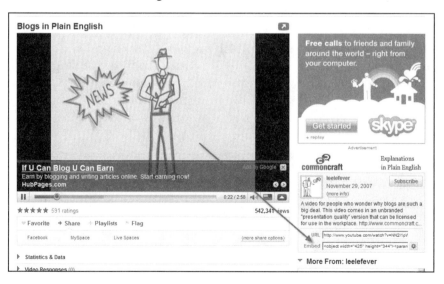

YouTube gives some options for styling the look of the video on a blog. You can choose size and color of frame. Make your choices, copy the embed code, and then go to your blog. In a new post, make sure you are using the HTML editor, and paste in the code. You can add comments, and then click to post.

Pay attention to copyright. Does the person who posted the video on YouTube hold the copyright on the video, and do you by implication have permission to repost?

Everyone has heard of YouTube, but have you heard of TED Talks (www.ted.com)? TED is an award-winning speaker series with outstanding speakers and both high educational and high entertainment values. I strongly encourage you to explore the TED Talks site. If you can find talks that fit into the subject of your blog, they are well worth posting. You can post them as long as your blog is not for commercial use. TED Talks also provides embed codes. Add this to your blog the same as with YouTube and voila! Instant fabulous content many of your readers have probably not yet seen.

Another example I like a lot is Slideshare. Slideshare (www .slideshare.net) is a site that allows people to share their presentation slides and audio. You can upload your presentations to Slideshare and get the embed code to repost easily to your blog.

Adding presentations and video to your blog is an effective way to boost the content. What better way to build compelling content than to include the work of brilliant storytellers and presenters and add your own commentary?

Creating a Blog Widget

Some widgets have been completely created for you, and all you need do is copy and paste the code into the correct spot on the blog. Other widgets have flexibility so that you can adjust them to suit you. If you are familiar with coding and development, you can also create your own widgets. Perhaps you will even share them with the larger community through Google or Yahoo!

For more examples, illustrations, and setup instructions for other widget options, such as Widgetbox Wizard, PollDaddy, and Google Countdown, see this book's companion wiki.

Meebo (www.meebome.com). Meebo is a tool for online chatting. It has a number of different uses, one of which is to create a chat box for your blog. This way, when you are online, people can see you are there and chat with you. A virtual reference service, if you will. The main Meebo site is www.meebo.com, but you must go to www.meebome.com to access the page to create your own Meebo chat (see Figure 3.12).

First, fill in your choices, and pick your color theme. Click on "Customize it . . ." to have even more color choices. Then you will need to sign up for a Meebo ID to complete the process and use your new chat box.

Be aware that if you are using this for true virtual reference, you may be unable to send hot links to Web sites to your readers. What a great way to get started to connecting with your readers, though, and testing out whether virtual reference is right for your library.

CAPTCHA. If your blog platform does not already have CAPTCHA capability, you can add it. CAPTCHA slows down spammers, especially those using bots as opposed to humans. Not all CAPTCHA applications are completely accessible. Some provide symbols that are difficult to read and do not give an audio alternative for those with visual impairment. I recommend ReCAPTCHA (http://recaptcha.net) for this purpose. Not only is it accessibility friendly, but it also repurposes your commenters' responses to clean up digitized documents—that is,

▶ Figure 3.12: Meebo Widget Maker on the Meebo Me Page (www.meebome.com)

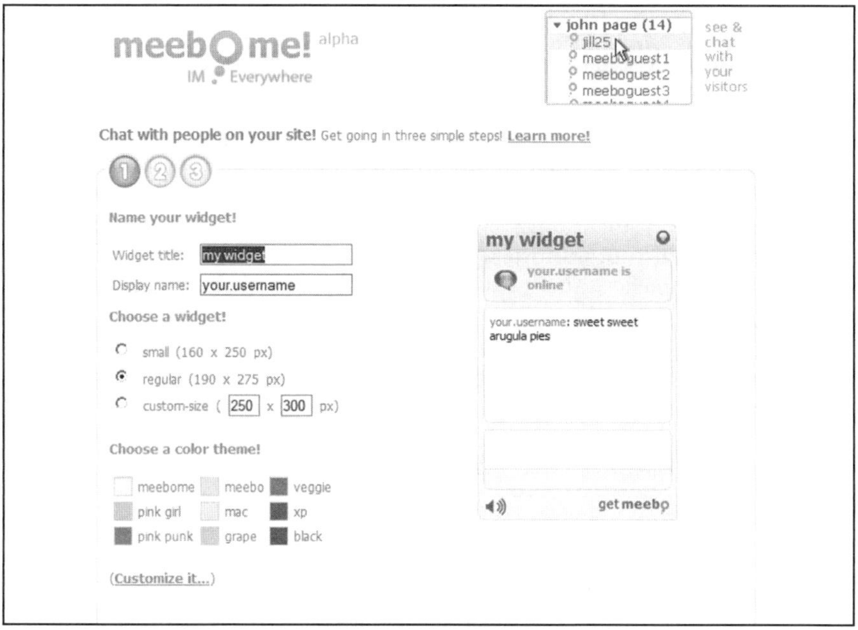

by typing in the words shown in the ReCAPTCHA graphics, they are helping transcribe digitized documents. This process is explained at http://recaptcha.net/digitizing.html.

Digg (http://digg.com). Digg is the social bookmarking Web site that allows you to share your favorites on the Web. If enough people "digg" what you have posted, it could show up on one of the main pages as a favorite.

To encourage people to "digg" your blog posts, Digg gives you a few tools. On the "Tools" page (http://digg.com/tools) scroll down to "For Website Owners & Developers." Here are a few options for you:

▶ The "Digg This" button (http://digg.com/tools/integrate) integrates into your blog. As people digg your site, you can have the little graphic update the count of the number of diggs for you.

▶ Add a Digg Widget (http://digg.com/add-digg) to your sidebar so that your Web site visitors see the latest Digg news.

▶ Digg Badges (http://digg.com/tools/buttons) are also available if you just want to manually add in the buttons for people to digg your stories. This is a lot more work, though.

Mobile Blog Versions

Many people are accessing the Internet using mobile devices these days, so it is a good idea to create a mobile version of your blog. Here are two tools to do this.

▶ **Winksite** (http://winksite.com): Winksite bills itself as being W3C compliant for mobile devices. You have to set up a free account before using it. To start, select which blog service you are using, and provide the blog feed URL. Note that they restrict you to creating five mobile sites, so if you have several blogs you may need to have more than one administrator create the mobile version. Winksite provides basic statistics such as number of visits to your site.

▶ **MoFuse** (www.mofuse.com): Another option is MoFuse. Go to "MoFuse for Blogs" at www.mofuse.com/a, and paste your blog URL into the box "Mobilize your blog now." MoFuse also gathers analytics so you can see how often your site is being accessed through a mobile device, and it can create a version of your blog for the iPhone.

iPhone Applications

iPhones are a little better at dealing with regular Web pages than some of the other mobile devices. Still, if you can create a version specifically for the iPhone, even better. MoFuse (www.mofuse.com) also creates an iPhone version when you create a mobile version (see previous section for details).

Dedicated Page for Widgets and Tools

If you have the ability to create pages, why not set up a page that explains your use of widgets and tools on the blog? This will inform your readers what has gone into the creation of the blog and give you a place to keep track of what has been done. It is also very helpful if you leave the blog administrator position and someone else takes over.

You may also talk about the widgets and tools in your main blog, but keep these types of posts to a minimum. Something like "we are trying out a new tool, let us know what you think" will probably suffice. Talking too much about the technology, unless the blog is technology focused, of course, will become boring and off-putting to much of your audience.

In the next chapter, you will discover ways to market your newly implemented blog in order to maximize its use and effectiveness.

▶4

MARKETING

▶ **Direct Traffic to Your Blog Site**
▶ **Join Blog Directories**
▶ **Employ Search Engine Optimization**
▶ **Send E-mail Notifications**
▶ **Engage in Social Networking**
▶ **Use Analog Techniques**
▶ **Submit Your Blog for Awards**

For some blogs you will want to get the word out to as many people as possible about the blog to attract as many visitors as possible. For others, such as reference desk blogs, the main point is communicating with a few people, not attracting large numbers of visitors.

▶ DIRECT TRAFFIC TO YOUR BLOG SITE

Content. Content. Content. This is the heart of any blog. Be sure you have good, original content that people enjoy reading. If they find your writing style engaging, they will return. Mix it up with photos and video in addition to written text. Write with lots of headings and bulleted lists to make posts easy for your readers to scan. Make titles more descriptive than clever, so people can find what they need later on when you have more than a few posts in the archives.

Once you get into a good routine of writing blog posts, try some of the following techniques to drive new traffic to your blog. Be aware, however, that people will not return if they do not find good quality posts when they get to your blog, so make sure you have the fundamentals down first. These techniques are for blogs on the Internet as opposed to internal blogs such as reference desk or departmental blogs.

Post a Top Ten List

American late night talk show host David Letterman popularized the "Top 10" list years ago, and people still can't get enough of them! Pull together an informative list for your readers with quick headings and some explanation. Those with blogs or Facebook profiles are more likely to share blog posts that are lists than other blog posts. Don't overstretch your content if you do not have ten items; if you only have seven great items, make it a "Top 7" list. Invite your readers to add to the list. I have seen lists that were "Top 5" easily increased to "Top 20" through reader input (see Figure 4.1).

Create a Link Love Post

This one walks a fine line ethically, so take care how you do it. A "link love" post is one in which you include a lot of people who are likely to link back to your blog post in return, thereby driving traffic from all of their blogs to yours. Generally speaking, it is a good idea to build in links to the Web sites of people who you are talking about, to give them some Web traffic. But if your sole purpose is to drive traffic back to your blog, take care. Creating a big list of people just so they will recip-

▶ Figure 4.1: Top 10 List of Top 10 Lists Posted on the Wellington City Libraries' Teen Blog (www.wcl.govt.nz/blogs/teens)

rocate and drive traffic back to your site can be seen negatively as "linkbait" and could create a backlash against you, causing others to question your blogging ethics.

This being said, if you can create a list that provides value and there happen to be people on the list who will pick up on it and link back to your site, then by all means post it. The key is to spend some time doing good evaluation of what you are putting together, categorizing things correctly, and giving readers value.

Compare these blog posts: Blake Carver discusses why each of the blogs was picked for LISNews' top blogs of 2008. LISNews chose a modest number (ten) and discussed each, explaining why the choices are relevant to the readers (see Figure 4.2). The Online College post also lists a number of blogs (a hundred!), with some explanation (see Figure 4.3). Unfortunately their details, such as categories and blog descriptions, are not always accurate. It appears as if the company that put the list together is trying to draw traffic to its new site to boost it in the Google search rankings; if those who are listed then link to this page, it will drive up their reputation immediately. Many of the bloggers listed in the second post have reacted quite negatively.

Hold Your Own Awards

People like to receive accolades and to be recognized. Why not start your own awards? Recognize those in your client or patron communities for things like best blogging in an industry, best Web site, or best fund-raiser (see Figure 4.4). Use your imagination as to what would ap-

▶ Figure 4.2: Blake Carver's "The LISNews 10 Blogs to Read in 2008" List (www.lisnews.org)

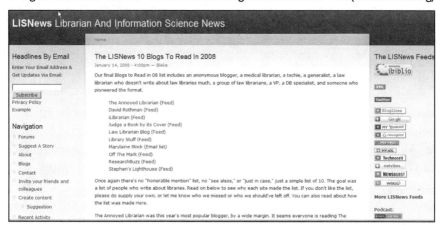

▶ Figure 4.3: Online College's "100 Best Blogs by School Librarians" (www.onlinecollege .org)

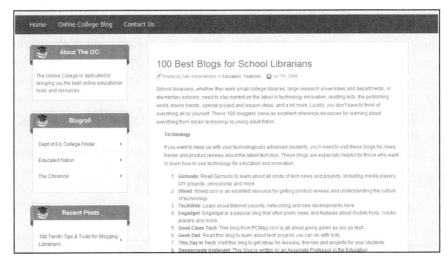

▶ Figure 4.4: The CLawBies—Canadian Law Blog Awards (www.clawbies.ca)

peal to your readers! What type of award hasn't already been created? Steve Matthews created the CLawBies, or Canadian Law Blog Awards, in 2006, and it has become a yearly tradition for Canadian law bloggers.

Create a badge that can be placed on the winners' blogs or Web sites. The HTML code for the badge should include the award logo (or other graphic), mention that the person is a winner (or even finalist/runner up), and a link back to your blog. When they place the code for the badge onto their sites, it will bring traffic and attention back to your Web site in addition to endorsing their own (see Figure 4.5).

Use StumbleUpon

StumbleUpon (www.stumbleupon.com) is a discovery tool that allows people to find new Web sites bookmarked by others. Firefox browser users can download a StumbleUpon toolbar that makes this process even easier than going to the Web site. When you see something you like, whether in StumbleUpon or not, you can recommend it to others. Add your blog posts. If someone discovers your blog and finds it compelling, he or she may come back.

Use Delicious

Delicious (http://delicious.com) is a social bookmarking site where people can also share what they have found. Emphasis is on tagging the content, so this site is good for researching. The more people have bookmarked any one site, the higher its relevance ranking will be in the search results. Bookmark your posts in Delicious.

People can also feed their Delicious findings out to other sites. For example, everything I bookmark is seen by my followers on the social networking site FriendFeed (www.friendfeed.com). You might also ex-

▶ Figure 4.5: 2008 CLawBies Badges and Code (www.clawbies.ca)

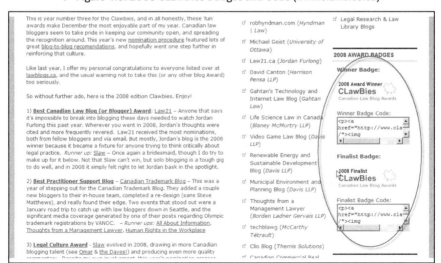

plore plug-ins or widgets for your blog that allow people to post to
Delicious.

Keep in mind that social networks aren't for running campaigns but
for building relationships with followers and friends and finding potential audience members of the blog. You can't just turn it on and
turn it off. It takes time. This is a
long-term tactic, so consider this
before you jump in with two feet.
You might want to just join
Facebook and observe what others
are doing first.

You can also use Digg (http://
digg.com) and Facebook (www
.facebook.com) to direct traffic to
your site. See Chapter 3 for more
details on both of these options.

Get Listed in Alltop

Alltop (http://alltop.com) bills itself as an "online magazine rack" di-
vided by popular topics. Once you are producing some solid content
on your blog, request to have it listed in the appropriate topic. For example, the Genealogy Alltop page (http://genealogy.alltop.com) currently includes the California Genealogical Society and Library Blog
(http://calgensoc.blogspot.com) and The Newberry Library Genealogy News (www.newberry.org/genealogy/news).

Comment on Other Sites

Adding comments to other sites is smart. It shows you are reading what
others are contributing and taking part in the blog community in your
subject area. Those people writing the blogs will likely have a look back
at your blog. It is also amazing how many of that blog's readers will also
have a look. So, it is a way to become known in that blog community. I
think of commenting to be similar to a tip in a restaurant: if you read a
blog post you appreciate, why not leave a comment to acknowledge
the thoughts and work of the blog author?

Set up a Google Alert for yourself so you see when others are mentioning or linking back to your blog. While Google Alerts don't pick up
100 percent of what gets posted to the Web, they will catch most in a
timely manner. When someone mentions your blog, pay attention. Is
there something you need to respond to in the comments? Keep in
mind that negative is okay; if someone is criticizing you it could be
because they care and want to see you do even better. If you have no
specific response, a note of thanks for the acknowledgment is appropriate.

When you comment, stay on point with the blog post topic. Ideally your comment should further the discussion at hand. So many times I get blog comments that say "Nice blog" or "Interesting discussion. I'll be back." I usually delete these comments from my blog. Why? Well, because their sole purpose is to provide traffic back to the person's blog. In other words, they are spam. There are people paid to go around to any number of blogs and drop in links in this way. In fact, there are "bots" on the Internet that can pick up on some of your text in the blog post and mimic a real comment for the sole purpose of building links back to a site. Keep this in mind—you don't want to appear like a spammer! It is okay to say something like: "Thank you, John. I appreciate all of the work you put into compiling this list and I will find it a useful resource." This is at least giving some feedback.

Guest Blog on Other Blogs

Guest blogging on another blog, ideally a higher profile blog, brings attention back to your organization. The trick is how do you become a guest? Cold-calling someone is not the answer. If you send someone you do not know a request to guest blog, you will probably be looked upon suspiciously. Your e-mail will be deleted without a response.

Approach only someone with whom you have built a relationship. Perhaps you already know a prominent blogger who is going on vacation? Or is busy and needs some new content? It doesn't hurt to offer. Ideally, someone invites you to guest blog.

Boost Your Blogroll

Add your favorite blogs on the subject to your blogroll. Hopefully those people will notice and visit your blog. If you are lucky, they will reciprocate and add you to their blogroll. (A lot of people don't update their blogrolls, though, so don't feel disappointed if they do not add you.) By putting some blogs of value together, you are also building a good resource for your readers, and this will hopefully bring them back directly to your site as well. Mention your blogroll in a post to encourage those reading your blog by RSS feed to visit you.

Create a Badge Advertising Your Blog

A badge is a type of widget. It is a small graphic with a link back to your Web site. Someone can grab a badge (or, rather, the code to create a badge) and drop it back on their own Web site or blog. Bloggers have badges on their blogs for all sorts of things: groups they belong to, groups they are supporting, events they are speaking at, events they are attending, publications, and other Web sites.

A badge can both advertise your library and drive traffic to your site. Put one of the badges on your own blog with a link from "Grab a badge" to a page with a few badge options and code for people to copy and paste onto their own sites (see Figure 4.6).

As an example, here is the full HTML code from one of the Cluttercast badges that you can use:

```
<a href="http://cluttercast.com/"><img src=
"http://cluttercast.com/images/badge_200x80.png"
alt="Cluttercast - Connecting through Clutter!"
/></a>
```

Because the image is housed on the Cluttercast.com Web site, if their logo changes they can change the image located in this file (giving it the same name), and the new image will show up on all the sites without new badges being needed.

Badges can be simple and professional or fun and whimsical. Decide what suits your audience best. Put them on your sidebar. Even better, put them on a separate page so that you can provide various versions without cluttering your front page.

▶ Figure 4.6: "Grab a Badge" from the Cluttercast Blog (http://cluttercast.com)

Widgets from Your Blog

Like badges at Cluttercast.com, you can create a widget (or blidget as it is called) at Widgetbox.com so that others can have your feed running on their site or blog. Again, post a link on your site to "grab a widget" and have the information on a separate page.

If you have other Web sites, post a widget from your blog to promote your posts. This is perhaps an easier way to pull in content from your blog than figuring out how to integrate an RSS feed.

Monitor Your Blog Statistics

Sophisticated bloggers know to check their blog statistics. You can see what blog posts are bringing in the most traffic and try to understand why. Was a recent post a "hit"? Or are your top posts those that have been on the site for a while? Sometimes if yours is the only blog addressing a very specific topic, it will pull up well in Google searches and bring a lot of traffic in over time.

Using blog post titles that describe the content with popular keywords will help the posts find the right audience through Google searches. Note what Google search strings are bringing in traffic. Do these make sense with regard to the audience you are aiming for? You may want to emphasis certain words more or less in your posts and blog titles. Blog statistics can also show you where traffic is coming from. Perhaps another prominent Web site has posted a link to one of your blog posts and that is bringing in traffic.

When you see what is giving you success, whether it is a specific post, Google search, or traffic from another Web site, you can adjust your future blog content to direct this a little more. Are people coming to your dog site with searches for corgis? Then write a feature post all about corgis. Statistics and blog metrics are described further in Chapter 6.

> Have a regular listen to the podcast "Marketing Over Coffee" (www.marketingovercoffee.com). Hosts John Wall and Christopher Penn are masters of marketing and share lots of ideas.

Place Mentions in Newsletters and E-mail Lists

If you know some e-mail lists, Google groups, e-mail newsletters, and even hard copy newsletters your audience is reading, do a little write-up for them about your new blog. Include the Web address so they can find you easily. Write it like a "call to action" that compels people to go to your blog. If the write-up is for an e-mail or an electronic newsletter, include a link in a prominent place, and tell people to click on it.

▶ JOIN BLOG DIRECTORIES

Don't just rely on Google! The more places you position your blog, the more likely it will be seen. And, because links from most other Web sites will help increase your ranking in Google searches, adding your blog to appropriate directories is a quick way to build up some status in Google as well.

Finding Blog Directories

You may be surprised at how many blog directories there are. For any given topic there can be dozens of directories. Start with some Google searching, and create a list for yourself. You will see that the caliber of blog directories varies immensely. Some feel "spammy," while others seem to hold some authority. It is amazing what a difference design and graphics can make in a blog directory.

Look at the submission criteria. Is it just a matter of giving them your URL and you are automatically added? Does your application have to go through an approval process? Many directories charge for you to be added. Unless they are well-known, you may want to turn to the paid directories as a last resort.

Narrowing Your Search

There are some "biblioblogosphere" directories where you can submit your library blog. In addition to those for libraries in general, look for ones about libraries in your subject area and also for subject-specific directories. Here are some places to start:

- ▶ **LISWiki—Weblogs** (http://liswiki.org/wiki/Blogs): This is a wiki, so you can add your blog into the appropriate location yourself.
- ▶ **The Blogging Libraries Wiki** (www.blogwithoutalibrary.net/links/index.php?title=Welcome_to_the_Blogging_Libraries_Wiki): This is another wiki you can add your blog to, or contact the wiki owner, Amanda Etches-Johnson, to be added.
- ▶ **LibWorm** (www.libworm.com): This is a library blog search engine. You must register first (this is free) to add your blog.
- ▶ **LISZEN—Library & Information Science Search Engine** (http://liszen.com): Add your blog by filling out the form at http://libraryzen.com/blog/?page_id=97.

▶ **LISZEN Wiki** (http://libraryzen.com/wiki/index.php?title=Main _Page): This wiki-based directory of blogs accompanies the LISZEN search engine. Add your blog (under LISZEN).

For general directories, look, for example, at Librarian's Internet Index (http://lii.org). Submit your blog via the form you find under "Suggest a site" at the top right of the page. Here are some other general blog directories to consider:

▶ **Technorati**: http://technorati.com
▶ **Blogcatalog**: www.blogcatalog.com
▶ **MyBlogLog**: www.mybloglog.com
▶ **Networked Blogs**: www.networkedblogs.com

Finally, look for blog directories that are specific to your subject area. An excellent example is the Law Library Blogs list (http://aallcssis .pbworks.com/Law-Library-Blogs) maintained by the American Association of Law Libraries' Computing Services SIS. You can request to be added or ask for access to the wiki and add yourself. Keeping with the law theme, Law X.0 (http://3lepiphany.typepad.com/3l_epiphany) has a category for law library and librarian blogs.

Even if you don't see a specific library category in the directories you have found, there are likely to be other categories you can fit into. Some directories will restrict you to be listed in one category, and others will let you add yourself to several. Take advantage of this, and add yourself to as many as are appropriate. Of course, don't overdo it, or, again, you will look like a spammer.

▶ EMPLOY SEARCH ENGINE OPTIMIZATION

Search engine optimization, or SEO, concerns setting up your Web site in such a way that it will pull up favorably in Web search engines, notably Google. It also involves giving your Web site other advantages such as links from outside sites so it will stand out from other sites during a search.

If you are looking for an external audience, spend time optimizing your blog as much as possible. Read what you can on the subject. Some experts who consult just on SEO alone can help with your site at a cost.

Google's Algorithm

Google's PageRank is an algorithm based on 200 indicators or "signals" to help determine where a Web site is weighted in search results. Google periodically changes its algorithm so that competitors cannot copy it and so that people cannot "game" the system to force their results to dominate. While we therefore cannot know exactly what the algorithm is or how to create our site to perform the best, some things do seem to affect rankings in Google:

- ▶ **Popularity**: If a site is already popular, it should remain popular and pull up well in many Google results.
- ▶ **Relevance**: Google looks seriously at how relevant the site is to the search in question. It is not enough to have some words embedded onto the page; they have to relate to the content of the site.
- ▶ **Recent content**: Google favors Web sites that are updated frequently. As a result, blogs that are updated often tend to do well in Google search results.
- ▶ **Links**: Google looks at how many links refer to the Web site. In particular, Google looks for links from sites that already have a good PageRank. The more authoritative the sites, the better your site will rank as well.

To check your Google PageRank, or the ranking of any Web site, paste the URL into the Page Rank Checker tool at www.prchecker .info/check_page_rank.php. If your site is pulling up at 5 or more (out of 10), you are doing very well. Very few sites rate a 7 or more.

Use Strong Keywords

You want to use words on your blog that pull up well in Google. You can add some in as meta-tags (tags that are coded into the HTML of the page but not seen by the Web site viewers), but this has gone by the wayside as the search engines ignore all but the first few. Putting keywords into the content, especially into post titles, is more effective.

You can try to come up with as many keywords as you can on your own, making as many iterations as possible. It is more efficient, however, to use an online tool that will generate keywords and give you an idea of how those words rank.

SEO Tools, for example, has an SEO Book Keyword Tool (see Figure 4.7). Plug in your words individually, and it will generate a number of keywords along with their relative values in the various search engine tools. This becomes particularly important when you get into ad-

▶ Figure 4.7: SEO Book Keyword Tool (http://tools.seobook.com/keyword-tools/seobook)

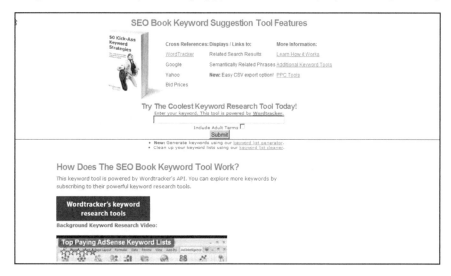

vertising with Google and on your personal blog (you probably wouldn't include advertising on a library blog).

For example, I plugged in the phrase "science fiction." These are the top ten phrases that came up:

1. Science fiction
2. Upcoming science fiction movies
3. Science fiction book club
4. Father of science fiction
5. Science fiction movies
6. Science fiction short stories
7. Science fiction channel
8. Science fiction novels
9. Science fiction art
10. Science fiction books

If you have a blog about science fiction, this gives you a pretty clear idea of what specific phrases to use to bring in traffic.

Beware Spam Practices

A number of so-called SEO experts will create fake blogs or other sites just to build links to the Web sites they have been hired to optimize.

These blogs are known as "splogs" (spam blogs). Such "experts" also set up directories, drop comments into blogs, generate blogs from random RSS feeds, and use many other tricks to build traffic for their customers. While few of these tactics individually have a lot of influence on Google, the spammers hope that by sheer volume their efforts will pay off.

You may run into some of these splogs in your travels of the blogosphere. If you hire someone to help with your blog, make sure that he or she does not participate in these practices. It is unethical and will make people (especially other bloggers) avoid your site.

Remember That Content Is King

The primary SEO method is to have good, solid content. Refresh it frequently with new blog posts. Google favors genuine human beings who write real content. Work in keywords where you can, but don't get hung up on every post being full of keywords. It has to all flow naturally. If a few of your posts one week don't hit these expectations, don't worry about it. The more you write on the topic, the more likely you are to naturally hit the good keywords. And, the better your content, the more likely those bigger, more influential Web sites will link to your blog posts.

▶ SEND E-MAIL NOTIFICATIONS

If your blog is internal, one way to get word out about new blog posts is e-mail notifications. Whether you do it manually or automate it, send out links back to the blog rather than reprint the full content.

If your department or library has an internal newsletter, include notes or links about the blog. Make it a "call to action"—write it so that people feel compelled to visit the blog or individual blog posts. It may seem silly, but inviting someone to "click the link to the see the full blog post" will actually get people clicking.

▶ ENGAGE IN SOCIAL NETWORKING

We've already talked at length about Facebook and social bookmarking type sites like StumbleUpon, Delicious, and Digg (in both Chapter 3 and earlier in this chapter). If there are any of these or others that you belong to, get the word out! Figure out where your audience is, tell them about your blog, and submit your blog posts for them to read. For many of these, you can automatically push out links to your fresh blog posts using tools such as Twitterfeed (http://twitterfeed.com).

For a more detailed discussion of employing social networking services in marketing, see this book's companion wiki. There you'll find information on such services as Twitter, Tumblr, FriendFeed, and MyBlogLog along with illustrations of their use in different library settings.

▶ USE ANALOG TECHNIQUES

Don't forget, all of the marketing techniques mentioned so far are in addition to traditional marketing techniques. Don't discount traditional methods, because they still work, just as TV advertising still works despite many predictions of its demise.

Flyers in the Library

Your library no doubt has some hard copy marketing and advertising materials. Why not include something about your blog? You can also create your own. A postcard-sized flyer works well and is easy to hand out. Of course there are always our favorites, the bookmarks. Either one can be tucked into books as you hand them to library clientele.

Face-to-Face Participation in Communities

Meeting the people you are serving is so important! The blog is meant to help you connect with them, not to replace face-to-face contact. Go to your community, where they meet, and take part. As yourself. Tell them about your blog. Use your blog to participate in the community: advertise their events; hold your own events for them; and advertise and record the events on the blog.

Yes, this is more public relations than marketing, but it is how you will get people to know you, your blog, your library, and the services you offer. And hopefully you will get to know the community you are serving even better, which can in turn develop into better services.

▶ SUBMIT YOUR BLOG FOR AWARDS

There are various awards available on the Internet for blogs and Web sites generally. Keep your eye out for these, and pay attention to whether you need to submit your blog to be eligible. Winning one or two awards looks good for your blog and brings some attention to you. Just Google "blog awards," and you come up with thousands! Here are a few big ones that typically take nominations:

▶ **The Weblog Awards** (http://weblogawards.org): Established in 2003, this is purportedly the world's largest blog competition with finalists in at least 45 categories (including general, topical, arts and letters, and international categories). Nominations begin in early November, voting is in December, and the awards are handed out in January.

▶ **Bloggies** (http://2009.bloggies.com): Nominations open January 1, finalists are selected in mid-January, voting takes place in late January, and winners are announced at the South by Southwest Interactive Festival in Austin, Texas, in mid-March of each year.

▶ **The BOBs** (www.thebobs.com): The BOBs are billed as "the world's largest international Weblog awards for Weblogs, podcasts, and videoblogs." Juried awards and people's choice awards are given to blogs currently in 11 different languages (and growing). They put out a call for nominations on international BlogDay, August 31; however, you can submit a blog at any time. Blogs do not have to be connected to any particular topic to participate. Winners are announced at the end of November.

▶ **Edublog Awards** (http://edublogawards.com): Also known as the "Eddies," these awards have a number of categories, including "Best group blog," "Best resource sharing blog," and "Best librarian/library blog." Nominations take place in November, voting takes place in the first half of December, and the awards are announced around December 20.

There are a lot of nationwide awards for various countries and subject-specific awards. As well, many organizations and individual blogs run their own awards. Take your pick as to which you best fit into. The smaller, more local the awards, the more likely you are to win. Some awards do require a submission payment, so keep an eye out for that and decide whether it is worth the submission cost. But it doesn't hurt to try the free ones! It is also helpful to look at past winners to see the caliber of the content and to get inspiration for your own blogs. Good luck! If you get more than one or two awards, you may need to create a page just to hold them.

Now we go into best practices for creating an effective blog as learned from some of the best bloggers.

▶5

BEST PRACTICES

- ▶ **Begin by Planning**
- ▶ **Ensure Accessibility**
- ▶ **Maintain the Blog**
- ▶ **Learn from Other Libraries' Experiences**

Let us review some of the best practices for effective blogging that we have looked at so far, compiled here for your convenience. Then we will take a closer look at lessons in effective (and ineffective) blogging practices that emerged from the questions I posed to the blogging libraries in my questionnaire.

▶ BEGIN BY PLANNING

To ensure an effective blog, it is important to plan by first answering some basic questions (for more on planning, see Chapter 2):

- ▶ Who is your target audience?
- ▶ What do you plan to communicate with the blog?
- ▶ Who is going to write it?
- ▶ What are you going to give up to make time for the blog?
- ▶ What type of software will you use?

Whichever type of blog software you choose, ideally have the blog on your own domain rather than on the software domain such as WordPress.com or Blogspot.com.

Once you've finalized your basic plan for the blog, move on to the particulars:

- ▶ **Create a schedule for posting**. Take into account how absences will be covered, both planned and unexpected. Posting should be a minimum of once a week, and ideally once a day.

▶ **Decide on a comment policy and post it.** This should address the type of comments considered unacceptable, how to deal with them, and whether you will moderate comments.

▶ **Make your blog design user-friendly.** See Chapter 3 for a full discussion of blog design requirements.

▶ **Validate your template code.** You can do this using http:// validator.w3.org.

▶ **Check your blog site in other browsers.** You should check as many other browsers as possible, both current and past versions.

▶ **Create a mobile version of your site.** Make your blog accessible by cell phones, iPhones, and other mobile devices.

▶ **Create a style guide for your blog.** This should outline branding elements that will be used consistently, such as the library name and logo consistently appearing in the same location with the same colors for text. Also, make sure the background and other design elements of the blog, such as font types and sizes, are the same.

▶ **Decide on a copyright policy and post it.** Your content can be fully copyrighted, have some limited rights reserved under Creative Commons, or be open for unlimited copy, reuse, and adaptation.

▶ **Add your site to general and subject-specific blog directories.** Look for free directories of good quality. Promote your site on social networks such as Facebook and Twitter, as well as in traditional ways such as with flyers, bookmarks, and mentions in your library newsletter.

▶ **Add a Web site statistics package to your site.** This will allow you to monitor traffic to your blog.

Features You Should Include in Your Blog

▶ Provide your readers both a link to your RSS feed and the ability to subscribe to updates via e-mail.
▶ Identify the bloggers, ideally with individual profiles.
▶ Create an About page.
▶ Ensure contact information can be easily found on the blog.
▶ Link back to your main Web site, and link from your main Web site to the blog.
▶ Include an archive of previous posts listed chronologically (ideally listed by month).
▶ Provide a search box to search for past blog posts.

▶ ENSURE ACCESSIBILITY

As much as possible, keep the blog simple (see Chapter 3 for more detailed discussion of accessibility best practices). Follow the recommendations of the W3C Web Accessibility Initiative (www.w3.org/WAI/

intro/accessibility.php). If you are in the United States, also follow the *Research-Based Web Design & Usability Guidelines* from the U.S. Department of Health and Human Services (www.usability.gov/pdfs/guidelines.html). This guide also references the Section 508 Web site (www.section508.gov/) from the IT Accessibility and Workforce Division of the U.S. General Services Administration.

Accessibility Best Practices

- ▶ Choose fonts and colors that people can read.
- ▶ Make links distinct from other text.
- ▶ Provide a text equivalent for all visual elements.
- ▶ Include captions, transcripts, and/or descriptions for all audio and video content.
- ▶ Write Web links using text that makes sense when read out of context.
- ▶ Use headings, lists, and a consistent structure (using CSS for layout if possible).
- ▶ Provide alternative content for widgets and plug-ins in case these features are not accessible or unsupported by a browser.
- ▶ Ensure that line-by-line reading in tables makes sense and summarize the table content.
- ▶ Try to go without CAPTCHA for preventing comment spam. If you must use it, ensure that you have an audio challenge as an alternative to the visual challenge.
- ▶ Organize sidebar elements with text titles, not images.
- ▶ Break your blog posts into paragraphs and use short, meaningful headings so that content is easy to scan.
- ▶ Use your blog software's feature for making lists rather than using asterisks or dashes.

▶ MAINTAIN THE BLOG

Make a conscious effort to keep staff interested in blogging. The blog should be sustained long term, when it is no longer a novelty. Also, monitor comments on the blog and respond to them. Decide in advance what you will do with negative comments. Pay attention to whether negative comments are actually trolls looking to be disruptive and get attention. Ensure blog post titles have some practical keywords in them for the purposes of giving you good search ranking on Google when people are searching for those words.

Monitor metrics such as number and quality of comments (both on the blog and received by other means), number of trackbacks, and number of mentions elsewhere on the Internet. Check your statistics package for blog traffic and related data. Monitor and record your Google's PageRank and number of links to your site on a regular basis.

▶ LEARN FROM OTHER LIBRARIES' EXPERIENCES

In October 2009 I sent out an informal questionnaire via Facebook, Twitter, FriendFeed, and a few e-mail discussion lists asking blogging libraries to discuss whether they consider their blogs to be successful and to explain what works and does not work. Of the 81 libraries with active blogs that responded, 45 felt their blogs were successful. Seven felt their blogs were unsuccessful, and there were an additional seven respondents whose blogs had become inactive or were closed. The rest with active blogs were either not sure if their blogs were successful or felt they had mixed success. The responses, amazingly, came from around the world and from all types of libraries, and yet some clear messages came through their collective comments.

A vast majority, including those with successful blogs, said they wanted to "blog more often" and do "more promotion." Other comments reveal what makes a library blog effective and ineffective:

Characteristics of an Ineffective Blog

- ▶ Buried on the library's Web site or intranet pages and therefore difficult for readers to find
- ▶ Comments that are not open, thereby limiting interactivity
- ▶ An unattractive site design
- ▶ Not maintained or updated (Two libraries cited difficulties working with Webmasters. One librarian mentioned she had started a blog but then found it was the wrong tool for what she was trying to achieve, which was creating a research guide.)
- ▶ Lack of comments on the blog posts (One respondent with a successful public library blog explained, "Blogs are about interaction so traffic's important but what we're really after is comments and discussion. I'd say we're marginally successful there as many of the comments are from other staff rather than external customers." Another from a school library wrote, "Since I work in a small school, people who read it are more likely to comment to me in person than they are to comment on the blog.")

Characteristics of an Effective Blog

- ▶ Writing with an informal tone (One public librarian said about his colleague's blog posts, "The voices are caring and authentic." Another said her library's blog kept "a friendly, approachable style.")
- ▶ Writing with multiple voices and styles.

- ▶ Getting as many of the library staff involved in writing the blog as possible (The adult service coordinator in a public library said they use a "rotating team of staff members to keep the blog fresh.")
- ▶ Adding photos to draw in readers (One school librarian said they even post photos of their students as a way to encourage the students to visit the blog.)
- ▶ Having space on the front page of the library or parent organization's main Web site (A number of libraries achieve this by feeding titles to the Web site with an RSS feed.)
- ▶ Updating the blog frequently and consistently with new content (Most successful blogs have a minimum of one new post a week; many add one new post a day. One law firm librarian explained that getting into the habit of posting was "more a matter of getting into the mind-set of always thinking 'how can I put this into a blog' so that . . . it became part of the normal working routine.")
- ▶ Having a professional-looking blog, including a clean typeface and using photos rather than clip art
- ▶ Archiving the blog posts by both date and subject or book genre
- ▶ Having a way for readers to sign up with e-mail subscriptions
- ▶ Providing "writing for the Web" classes for the staff (One large public library that has over 20 blogs spreads the blogging over 20 to 30 people and teaches "classes for staff on how to write for the Web and to get participation.")
- ▶ Making one or two staff members responsible for overseeing the blog to ensure consistency
- ▶ Adding it to staff members' job descriptions (One public library explained that "having staff post as part of their formal jobs" is the one thing they would not change with their successful blog.)
- ▶ Setting up a support system for the bloggers, with a focus on new bloggers (One public library with a number of successful blogs says it has "a diverse group of trained and supported bloggers. We have grown our blogger pool over the couple of years it's been going and are set up to deal with the tentative new blogger, through Web team support, right through to the frequent and experienced blogger.")

Effective Blog Features

- ▶ Book reviews (about older books in addition to the new ones)
- ▶ Links to book and movie Web sites
- ▶ Feeds to social networks, such as Facebook and Twitter
- ▶ Photos from library-hosted events
- ▶ Guest—including library client—posts
- ▶ Video blog posts

Keep in mind success is often in the eye of the beholder. Especially if you serve a focused clientele or are blogging on a niche topic, it is less about how many people you reach and more about reaching the right people. If you are expecting many hits and comments, you may be disappointed. Soliciting comments on a blog is particularly difficult and varies depending on the culture of a group or organization. According to research performed by Charlene Li and Josh Bernoff for *Groundswell* (www.forrester.com/groundswell), commenters—those in their "Critics" category—is the second highest level of engagement on the Internet, second only to content creators, but it is still only 39 percent. Regardless of demographic, the reality is that most blog readers are not inclined to comment.

A children's services manager in a public library said she would "continue to encourage staff to be innovative in posting." Certainly trying out different types of posts and other new tactics and seeing what works will help to keep the blog vital and therefore successful. Pay attention to popular blogs in other areas to see what is working for them.

How to Promote a Blog

Promoting the blog more was at the top of most respondents' list of things to improve. These ideas worked for the responding libraries:

> ▶ Posting headlines or full blog posts to the front of the organization's main Web site
> ▶ Mentioning the blog in classes run by the library and other departments
> ▶ Linking to the blog from educational software such as Moodle
> ▶ Including the blog URL on paper materials such as bookmarks and newsletters
> ▶ Including the blog in traditional advertising from the library

A number of people mentioned they wanted to try contests as a way to drive traffic to the Web site. However, a number who tried this found that it was not effective at bringing in new readers.

As with any public relations campaign, the goal should be to gradually build a strong following, and ideally relationships with your readers, over time. It will take work to get word out. Promote it on a number of fronts and keep doing so. Success will not be overnight, but will come in increments.

How to Determine Success Rate

I asked the respondents how they determine the success of their blogs. Most referenced measurements such as these:

- ▶ Traffic to the Web site, expressed as number of hits on the site, measured with a statistical software package such as Google Analytics
- ▶ Number of subscribers to the blog's feed
- ▶ Number of comments on the site
- ▶ Number of links from other sites
- ▶ Amount of anecdotal evidence and comments via e-mail, face-to-face discussions, and at the reference desk

While having a high volume of traffic to the site or a large number of comments is a clear indicator that the site is doing something right, what happens if you do not receive much in the way of traffic or comments? Many of the respondents expressed disappointment that they did not receive the traffic and especially the number of comments they had hoped, but they identified some additional ways that they determine the success of their blogs:

- ▶ Number of times books featured on the blog were reserved or signed out
- ▶ A spike in traffic to the blog when certain events were featured or when the blog post tied in to a specific service
- ▶ Response to questions about the blog in library user surveys
- ▶ Engagement of readers with the blog outside the blog itself
- ▶ Positive feedback from staff in the library's parent organization, including being used as a model by others
- ▶ Number of mentions in the parent organization's internal and external communications
- ▶ Number of readers and subscribers increasing over time
- ▶ Volume of traffic received from Facebook and Twitter, especially if links were posted on these sites originally by the library
- ▶ Number of times the blog post was posted to Facebook and retweeted on Twitter
- ▶ Older blog posts on the site continuing to receive significant traffic when measured against more current posts
- ▶ The path visitors to the site make through the site—whether they spend a significant length of time on the site and move to additional pages

Most important, they looked at success in terms of whether the blog met their original goals, regardless of the hits on the blog, for example:

- ▶ The blog is useful for reader advisory support. A respondent from a public library explained: "We index entries by genre rather than date and can use these reviews to assist patrons with Advisory questions, so even if we don't have a wide readership, it serves a purpose."

▶ The blog has replaced other forms of communication, such as news-letters or e-mail, representing increased efficiency. One library manager in a private organization said, "We can share information that used to go out in e-mails. When it went in an e-mail you had to figure out where to save it because you may want to refer to it again. Now it goes on the blog which can be searched. It is efficient, saves time and I know it is used, both for the current and as an archive."

▶ Other library staff members are becoming informed as to news and information posted to the blog, and reference staff is increasingly informed. A respondent from a large public library proudly explained, "Most staff refer to the blog to know what is going on in the library. It is a useful tool for a place that is open 70 hours a week and that employs many part-timers. Communicating across different shifts can be challenging and we've met that challenge!"

▶ The quality and depth of posts allows reference staff to refer clientele with questions to specific blog posts. One academic library staff member said, "Many of the posts are considered to be of high enough instructional quality that we sometimes refer reference questions to a blog post."

▶ The blog has had a good impact on the library's or parent organization's culture. For example, one special librarian mentioned, "Blogging makes the employees more Web 2.0 minded." Similarly, a public librarian said, "The biggest success element has been the fact that it provides a creative outlet for staff, both professional and paraprofessional."

The last word goes to one particularly eloquent respondent from a public library:

> "A successful blog is one in which it can be integrated smoothly into the everyday workflow of the library staff, at the same time providing useful information to the [clientele group] in a new and exciting way. The time it takes to maintain it should reflect the amount of hits and subscription to the blog, but perhaps not initially. . . . The blog must be sustainable, as well, not leaving the task of posting to one person, but having ownership among staff so that it can be continually kept up."

The last step in creating an effective blog is measuring its success. Once we know how to quantify results, which is discussed in Chapter 6, we can then figure out ways to improve it.

▶6

MEASURES OF SUCCESS

- ▶ Add Analytics Measurement Software
- ▶ Check Your Google Ranking
- ▶ Track Links to Your Site
- ▶ Review Comments and Feedback
- ▶ Monitor Blogosphere Discussions and Trackbacks
- ▶ Use Social Bookmarking Tools

How many people are reading your blog? Who are they? How did they get to your blog? What is driving traffic to your blog? Who is talking about your blog? And, does it really matter? Bloggers tend to pay attention to a lot of the metrics associated with their blogs, whether for business purposes, an ego boost, or just plain curiosity. Tracking statistics is also important for measuring how effective, useful, and popular your blog is.

However, it is easy to lose sight of just which statistics are important. Is it important to have a lot of readers? What about readers who only visit your site once, do not comment, and never return? Perhaps it would be better to have fewer people stop by on a regular basis and become engaged in talking with your library. Businesspeople often talk about measuring "return on investment," but perhaps it is better to talk in terms of "return on influence." This is really what you want to know: does your blog have an impact on the services you provide and on the number of people who find your services?

▶ ADD ANALYTICS MEASUREMENT SOFTWARE

One of the first things you should do is add analytics measurement software to your blog. This will allow you to see your progress in bringing readers to the site from the beginning. Analytics software tracks statistics such as how many people have visited the Web site, how often, for how long, and how many pages they viewed. It can tell you a number of other things as well, such as which pages are most popular and which Google searches were used to reach your Web site. It can keep track of where people come from, getting fairly specific although not usually telling you who exactly was looking at your site. You can see what countries and sometimes cities they came from and what browsers and operating systems they use. With some software, you can get specific enough to see one individual's path through your Web site as well.

Generally speaking, you will want to look at the statistics aggregated rather than tracking individuals unless you notice a problem visitor (such as a spammer) on your site. Looking at the big picture will give you a better idea as to what is popular, what is bringing in traffic, and which links to you are bringing traffic your way. You can then use this information to adjust your content and keywords to improve your ranking on Google.

Some of the blog platforms, such as WordPress, include simple statistics; however, while these may be fun for hobby bloggers, they are unlikely to be sufficient for your purposes. I recommend you link to a separate package from your site.

This section looks at some popular analytics software packages. Probably the best known is Google Analytics, and it is free. FeedBurner (described last) is the only one that monitors statistics from your feed and so should be used in conjunction with one (or more) of the others. You may also want to use more than one of the others, too, to compare for accuracy. They have been known to come up with different results.

All of these packages reside "in the cloud"; that is, the statistics are gathered on the software companies' Web sites, often with the option for you to download stats to your own spreadsheet package. They all monitor usage on the Internet; if you are using internal blogs for your organization, check with your intranet administrator for similar analytics software for inside the firewall.

Some of the packages will require you to place a link from your blog site. Also keep an eye out for plug-ins; for example, there is a WordPress plug-in for Google Analytics. When you set them up, look for a way so that you can opt out of counting your own visits (and that of other blog administrators) into the analytics. You will be on the site more than anyone, so your visits could significantly sway results.

Think about whether you want to post number of visitors to your site on the site itself. While it is fun to watch the meter climb, I'm not sure it lends anything to your visitors' experience and it may even be harmful. If they don't know that you are just starting out, they could wonder why you don't have more visitors. This may influence them to not return.

SiteMeter (www.sitemeter.com): SiteMeter is one of the original Web site analytic software packages and, as a result, is very popular. Recent reviews, however, have not been exactly favorable. SiteMeter has a free and a paid level. At the free level you can track basic metrics, including details of the last 100 visitors to your site.

Go to SiteMeter's demo page (www.sitemeter.com/?a=samplestats) to find out what is available for free. You must put a visible link to SiteMeter on your Web site to use the free version.

The free level of this product may be sufficient for you in the beginning but not enough for your ongoing tracking. If you like the service, upgrade to the premium (paid) level for these additional features:

▶ The path taken by visitors to your site
▶ The Web page that referred the visitor to your site
▶ How long the visitors stayed on the site
▶ Search engine keywords people used to find your site
▶ The domain of the Web site that referred most of your last 4,000 visitors to your site
▶ Rankings of Web sites, Web pages, and search engines that have referred visitors to your site
▶ An invisible meter so that your blog visitors do not see a mention of statistics being gathered
▶ Ability to export details of the last 4,000 visitors to a CSV or text file to perform your own statistical analyses

You can also explore the premium statistics features on SiteMeter's demo pages (www.sitemeter.com/?a=samplestats).

There have been concerns as to whether SiteMeter has been adding spyware cookies to client Web sites. These concerns were raised by a number of sources in 2007, at which time SiteMeter responded that they were testing new features that would give client Web site owners more information about their site visitors. If this is of concern to you, you may wish to use one of the other analytics software packages mentioned here.

StatCounter (www.statcounter.com): StatCounter, like SiteMeter, has a free level as well as various paid levels, depending on how many statistics you would like to see aggregated over time. The free level tracks the last 500 visitors to your site. StatCounter's free level also gives you largely the same features as the paid level, so it is sufficient for getting you started.

Statistics can be presented in different graphical formats, such as bar graph, area graph, or no graph. Data can be shown daily, weekly, monthly, quarterly, and yearly, with time spans that are adjustable (see Figure 6.1).

Overall I find StatCounter to be far more sophisticated than SiteMeter. It provides a lot more breakdown of the data, even when you compare StatCounter's free level to SiteMeter's premium level.

▶ Figure 6.1: StatCounter Blog Statistics for Connie Crosby's Blog

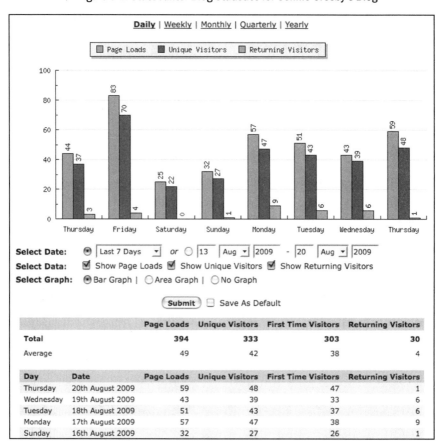

	Page Loads	Unique Visitors	First Time Visitors	Returning Visitors
Total	**394**	**333**	**303**	**30**
Average	49	42	38	4

Day	Date	Page Loads	Unique Visitors	First Time Visitors	Returning Visitors
Thursday	20th August 2009	59	48	47	1
Wednesday	19th August 2009	43	39	33	6
Tuesday	18th August 2009	51	43	37	6
Monday	17th August 2009	57	47	38	9
Sunday	16th August 2009	32	27	26	1

You can also use just one statistics package from StatCounter to track multiple sites. You will have to decide how many users you are going to track for each site with your existing allotment and set it to track them. If you are tracking more than one site, it is probably worth going up to a paid level to give you more aggregated statistics. For example, you can see which page was most popular by the last number of visitors you have designated. The higher the number, the clearer a picture you will get of overall trends.

Google Analytics (www.google.com/analytics): To many, Google Analytics is all you will ever need. It is sophisticated, powerful, and—best of all—free.

For all its benefits, some people find it overwhelming and too difficult to use. This makes sense because Google aims their package at marketers and provides data to help track things like success of ad campaigns. At the same time, others complain that it does not give the in-depth detail and tracking that StatCounter does. So, it will depend on how much detail and what kind of detail you need whether Google Analytics is the solution for you.

FeedBurner (http://feedburner.google.com): One of the main reasons to set up your RSS feed with FeedBurner is for its metrics. This tool will tell you how many are subscribing to your feed. Otherwise, this is a missing piece of the data and possibly significant depending on how many in your audience are not going directly to your Web site but are instead using feed aggregators to read your content.

To set it up, simply copy your RSS feed URL and paste it into the "Burn a feed right this instant" box. Add the resulting feed to your Web site instead of the original feed so that your readers use the FeedBurner feed (see Figure 6.2).

The FeedBurner screenshots show you the recent statistics for the feed I set up for the Community Divas podcast (a show I record with Eden Spodek). It shows number of subscribers and how many people accessed the feed. It appears we are still gathering new subscribers despite being on hiatus; most subscribers are not currently coming through iTunes but through various Internet sites (notably FriendFeed) because new episodes are not currently being pushed out. Trying to understand why you see certain activity is part of the fun of monitoring your metrics!

▶ Figure 6.2: FeedBurner Statistics on Number of Subscribers and People Accessing Community Divas' RSS Feed

▶ CHECK YOUR GOOGLE RANKING

How your blog ranks in Google searches will influence how much Web search traffic will find your blog. Your weighting in Google searches is expressed as a Google PageRank. To check your PageRank, have a look at the Google Page Rank Checker from PRChecker.info at www .prchecker.info/check_page_rank.php. Of a possible 10, anything 5 or over is considered good weighting on Google. Very few sites garner a weighting over 7. The higher your PageRank, the more influential you are considered to be and the higher your blog will turn up in Google search results.

▶ TRACK LINKS TO YOUR SITE

Another measure of the influence of your blog is how many sites link to it. There are at least two ways to do this: search for links on Google or use the Yahoo! Site Explorer tool. Your main reason for taking part in the community is to build interest in the programs and services of the library. Keep this in mind. It is not always just about the number of links!

Google Search for Links (http://google.com): To use Google search, type in the search string "link:URL" without the quotes. For example, let's pretend we administrate the California State Library Blog and plug in "link:blog.library.ca.gov."

Figure 6.3 shows 259 links to the blog. If you look through the results, you see a number of these are the blog referencing itself, which is perfectly fine. Hopefully over time the blog will garner more links from outside sources. This is one of the reasons why being active within the related blog community can be important. If they talk about you frequently you will soon build up additional links.

Yahoo! Site Explorer (https://siteexplorer.search.yahoo.com): This tool will allow you to explore the links a little more thoroughly and includes badges and other features that advanced users and developers might find of interest. Paste your blog site URL into the box at the top of the page, and click "Explore URL." A list of all your pages and individual blog posts is created. Then click on the button marked "Inlinks." The number in parentheses next to "Inlinks" is the number of links to your site.

Again using the California State Library Blog as an example, compare the numbers of links identified. Note the large difference. Yahoo! brings up a lot more (see Figures 6.4 and 6.5). This tool also has the option of viewing links to "Only this URL" (i.e., the homepage) or to "Entire site." I suggest checking the entire site unless there are spe-

▶ Figure 6.3: Google Search Results Showing Links to the California State Library Blog

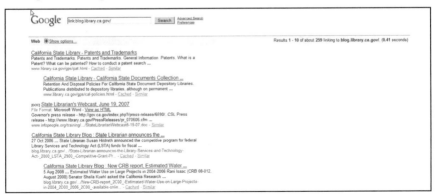

▶ Figure 6.4: Searching for Links to the California State Library Blog Using Yahoo! Site Explorer

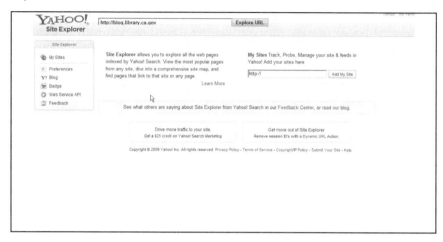

▶ Figure 6.5: Yahoo! Site Explorer Search Results Showing Links to the California State Library Blog

cific pages you want to check. You can also obtain additional metrics if you authenticate your site with Yahoo. This involves adding a meta-tag to your site and having them crawl your site.

Feed Reader Subscribers

Using FeedBurner (described earlier) helps you monitor how many visitors from feed readers you have. Some of the readers have their own ways of checking the number of subscribers for your blog as well—I will discuss three popular ones. You may note some discrepancies between these and FeedBurner's counts, which is why you may want to look into these in addition to FeedBurner. Because your subscribers can be using other aggregators, including desktop readers and mobile readers, just measuring feed readers won't give you a complete count of subscribers.

Google Reader (www.google.com/reader): Currently Google counts subscribers from the feed reader Google Reader together with the build-it-yourself homepage iGoogle. A simple way to see how many are subscribing to your feed is to open a Google Reader account and subscribe to your own feed. Open the feed, click on the "Expanded" view option, and then ask it to "show details" (both options are toward the upper right of the Reader). Near the top it will give you number of subscribers (see Figure 6.6).

To use a more sophisticated method, sign up for Google Webmaster Tools (www.google.com/webmasters), a companion software package to Google Analytics. First set up a Google Account if you don't already have one. Then add your site under "Add a site." Last, you have to verify your site by adding a meta-tag to your site (some code added to the HTML code of your Web site that your readers will not see). If you have created your blog with Blogger, this can be done directly from the Blogger dashboard.

▶ Figure 6.6: Number of Google Readers Subscribing to Connie Crosby's Blog

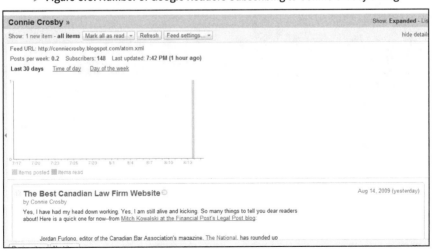

Bloglines (www.bloglines.com): Like Google, Bloglines has an easy way and a more sophisticated (i.e., more difficult) way to see your number of subscribers. The easy way is to add a feed. After you do this, Bloglines will come back with additional information about your feed, including number of subscribers (see Figure 6.7).

When I check mine, I discover two different numbers. That is because Blogger actually has two types of feeds: RSS and Atom. You can see I have 178 subscribers via Bloglines. You can check anyone's number of subscribers this way.

In the more sophisticated method, under "Account," select "Publisher Tools" and then "Begin Claim" under "Claim a Feed." Follow the instructions; these will differ depending on the blog platform you are using. Once you have completed the claim and verification process, you will be shown your number of subscribers. Those on the Blogger platform may experience some problems in successfully verifying your blog feed; it would not give me access, and others have unfortunately reported the same problem.

▶ REVIEW COMMENTS AND FEEDBACK

Keep track of the comments on your blog plus any off-blog feedback you receive, such as via e-mail or in person. Start a spreadsheet, and designate someone to keep track each week. Crunch the numbers and

▶ Figure 6.7: Connie Crosby's Blog Statistics on Bloglines

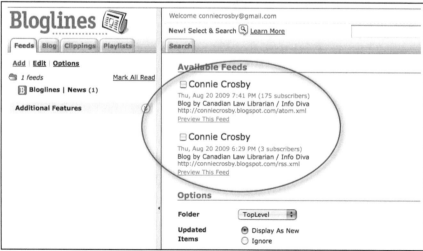

watch your progress over time. This begins to be most interesting when your blog has been published for some time and you have a larger set of data to aggregate. You will begin to see trends and, hopefully, increasing numbers.

In addition to simply measuring the number of comments a blog receives, in his book *The Liblog Landscape 2007–2008*, Walt Crawford (2009) suggests also measuring "conversational intensity," or number of comments per post. Conversational intensity is found simply by taking the number of posts and dividing it by the number of comments on the blog within a given time period. This helps compare different time periods in which number of posts (and therefore number of overall comments) may vary.

Remember that number of comments is not everything. It is more about quality of readership, whether you are hitting your target market, and whether people are actually staying on and reading the site. Some audiences are not inclined to post comments. If you are hearing, however, that people are talking about the blog and sending comments via e-mail, you know you are reaching them. For a library blog, pay more attention to quality than to quantity. You are not out to make money on the blog; you are using it to provide service and/or highlight your library's other services.

▶ MONITOR BLOGOSPHERE DISCUSSIONS AND TRACKBACKS

Along this same line, it is not necessarily how many mentions you receive out on the Internet, but whether you are reaching the bloggers and Web site owners in your target audience and the quality of their links to you. It is preferable for them to be engaging in thought leadership and responding to your content than for you to be one of hundreds of links on their blogrolls.

It is a good idea to regularly search the Internet for mentions in the "blogosphere." Also, watch the trackbacks on your individual blog posts to see how many people are linking to you. Trackbacks, remember, are links from other blogs to your blog post. Often blog platforms allow you to set them up so that these links show along with any comments. Some, like WordPress, show you incoming links from the administrative back end.

There are a few tools useful for checking your mentions in the blogosphere: Technorati, Google Blog Search, and IceRocket. For the latter two, once you run a search, you can take the RSS feed created and watch the comments via your feed reader rather than having to run searches regularly. There are huge overlaps in the results found with these tools; none, unfortunately, is comprehensive.

Ideally you should check these on a continuous (daily) basis so you can respond to discussions as they happen. It is probably more realistic, however, to have someone check once a week or as often as possible.

You may get a few "bad" results: blogs full of links meant to up someone else's search engine ranking (these are called spam blogs or "splogs") and blog posts with automatically generated links to supposedly related blog posts on other sites. There is nothing really wrong with the latter, but they are not high-quality links and there is not a lot for you to respond to with these. If there is a vehicle for reporting spam blogs to the blog host, I do so.

You are going to do three things with these metrics:

1. Keep track of number of links and conversations.
2. Respond to the conversations when appropriate.
3. Check those who are linking to you to see whether they are influencers with your potential audience.

Technorati (http://technorati.com): Technorati is a service that indexes many of the blogs on the Internet. For best results, join Technorati and submit your blog. Then you can search from the search page (http://technorati.com/search) using your URL, and you will pull up results specific to your blog.

Technorati search results also show you its authority rating of each blog on a scale of 0 to 1,000. The higher the authority number, the more authority Technorati considers the blog to have. You can search results by authority level of the blog (highest authority first) or by "freshness." This is not a comprehensive search because Technorati does not pick up all blogs, but it will likely pull up links you will not find with the other tools.

Google Blog Search (http://blogsearch.google.com): On Google's Blog Search page, paste in your blog URL, and you will see recent links to your blog. The search results include links from blog posts, from blogrolls on the blog site, and "related links" automatically generated. The search generates an RSS feed (in the sidebar on the left). Use this to monitor your search results with a feed reader.

IceRocket (www.icerocket.com): In the blog's search box, type in "link:" and the URL of your blog without spaces. For example, I searched for links to the Library of Congress Blog by typing in link:loc .gov/blog. The results are shown in Figure 6.8. Compared with searches using other tools, IceRocket shows a lot of duplication, and it has picked up a lot fewer blog posts. However, it seems to pick a few more links from individual blogs (i.e., when another blog has mentioned the Library of Congress Blog in multiple posts), a few different "related links" generated automatically, and one or two other posts not previously found. It is also worth registering for an IceRocket password to explore some of its other services, such as BlogTracker and Trend Tool.

▶ USE SOCIAL BOOKMARKING TOOLS

Don't just post links to social bookmarking sites such as Delicious, Digg, and StumbleUpon; check how many other people are bookmarking your site! Monitoring once a month is probably sufficient, because you won't be responding to anyone. However, if you have someone monitoring the blogosphere once a week, why not do this at the same time on a weekly basis? This way it becomes a routine and hopefully is less onerous for the person monitoring.

There are a few things you want to take away from this activity:

1. Monitor how many people are bookmarking your blog site (that is, the main domain).

▶ Figure 6.8: IceRocket Search Results for the Library of Congress Blog (http://loc .gov/blog)

2. Monitor how many people are bookmarking individual blog posts and how this trends through time.

3. Pay attention to those blog posts that rate highly (i.e., get bookmarked the most often), learn from those posts, and try to create more like them.

4. Note how people have tagged your site, and try to use those tags and keywords in blog titles to attract these same people back.

Here is how you find out the number of times you have been bookmarked in some of the popular social bookmarking sites:

Delicious (http://delicious.com): You will need a Delicious account to monitor all the blog posts. Once you bookmark a page or an entire site, Delicious tells you how many others have saved the same site (see Figure 6.9). You can also search for number of links from the URL search page (http://delicious.com/url).

Delicious reports how many people have saved the site, how many notes were written, who first bookmarked the site, and when it was first bookmarked. On the right of the screen it shows how people have tagged the site. Study the ones used for your site. Have people tagged it the way you would have? Their tags can give you new ideas for keywords to use in your titles. With Delicious you can also view the individuals' profiles (which are unfortunately somewhat minimal on this service) and their other links and add them into your network.

Digg (http://digg.com): Digg's focus is on "news" content, so you may see fewer bookmarks with this site than with Delicious. If you are very fortunate, someone else has already submitted your site or blog

▶ Figure 6.9: The Library of Congress Blog Bookmarked on Delicious

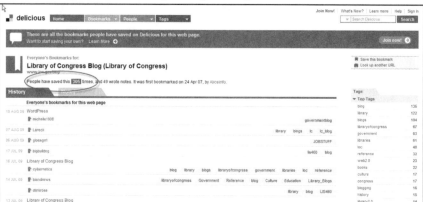

post, and all you need to do is monitor how many votes or "diggs" it receives. Find this by searching for the blog post URL or the name of the post. Don't forget to digg it yourself! That extra vote can't hurt.

For example, a number of people have submitted posts from the Library of Congress Blog (see Figure 6.10). A few have "dugg" these pages. You can see when these were first submitted although not to which category. When checking your site, note how others have described the page and whether they have cribbed a summary from your post or written their own.

As with Delicious, you can also submit your own page. It will look for duplicates in the system first, and if not already found it will add your submission. You can include a description and, if you have images on your site, choose an image (a "thumbnail") to represent your submission. You will be asked to place your submission in one subject area. As a librarian, I always find this difficult because there is no way to cross-index over several topics! Do your best and choose the one that suits your blog post. One idea is to place it in the subject area that your audience fits into. If they are checking subject-specific pages, hopefully they will see your post there.

If you build up a network of friends on Digg, invite them to digg your post as well. Don't forget to reciprocate by voting for some of the things they are posting as well!

StumbleUpon (www.stumbleupon.com): Again, you can search to see if anyone has bookmarked your site (be sure to select "search"

▶ Figure 6.10: Library of Congress Blog Listing on Digg

rather than "stumble," which is random and will take you to one site). To submit your blog, register for and sign in to a StumbleUpon account. Ideally you should set up the toolbar for yourself in the browser. Then go to your blog page and click on the "thumbs up" page to add it to your favorites. Once it is in Your Favorites, you can see how many other reviews your blog has received. If you are using the Firefox toolbar, click on the "Info" button in the toolbar to see the reviews.

Note not only the reviews, including comments, but also the "People who like this" on the right. If you move your cursor over their photos you will find out more information about them. You can also click on their photos to see their other favorites.

This book has given you a fairly comprehensive look at blogging for libraries. Take a step back, and consider the essentials:

- ▶ Do blogs fit into your library's overall marketing, communication, or service delivery strategy? Would it help to achieve your organizational or departmental goals?
- ▶ Who is your audience?
- ▶ What will you blog about?
- ▶ Who will write the posts?

Having relevant and up-to-date content is really the best key to success. The rest comes down to personal and organizational preferences. If you are very new to this, begin with a small personal blog just to try out the technology, see how things function, and work out the kinks.

Remember, whatever you choose to do with your blog, it is meant to be *fun*. Don't lose sight of that! Take advantage of this to be creative and produce something lively that your audience will find engaging.

GLOSSARY

aggregators: Also known as "feed readers," "news readers," or simply "readers," these are tools for reading RSS feeds such as those provided by blogs, news sources, and Google Alerts.

Atom: A type of feed from blogs, coded in XML. These feeds can be read with an aggregator or fed onto a Web page for viewing. RSS is another, similar format.

badge: A type of widget for your blog, usually with a static message, such as an advertisement for an event that links to another Web site.

biblioblogosphere: All library-related blogs; also, the community of library-related blogs.

blog carnival: A special type of blog post summarizing the previous week's (or two weeks') worth of best blog posts on the Internet on a specific subject or theme. What makes it carnival-like is that it moves around from blog to blog and is therefore collectively authored by many bloggers.

blogosphere: All blogs; also, the blogging community.

blogroll: List of blogs read by the blogger, often listed in the sidebar of the blog Web site.

CAPTCHA: A challenge (usually difficult-to-read text) that quizzes us to see if we are human or an automated bot on the Web spreading spam. It can also come in the form of an audio challenge or a puzzle to be solved. CAPTCHA stands for Completely Automated Public Turing test to Tell Computers and Humans Apart.

categories: A predetermined list of subject headings or keywords (in other words, an authority list) used to index individual blog posts.

CMS: *See* CONTENT MANAGEMENT SYSTEM.

comment policy: Policy created by the blog owner outlining what types of comments are unacceptable and describing what actions will be taken by the blog's owner if inappropriate comments are posted. It may also include a disclaimer stating that comments of commenters do not necessarily reflect the blog owner's opinions.

comments: A feature of blog software that allows readers to add comments to individual blog posts.

content management system: Also known as a CMS, a computer platform that allows for updating and management of Web content, whether on a Web site or an intranet, that is easier than using HTML coding.

CSS: The coding for a Web site that creates the style elements for the site, such as colors and fonts. CSS stands for cascading style sheets.

header: The top of the blog Web site containing the blog title, similar to the masthead of a newspaper.

hex: Short for "hexadecimal," this is a numeric value, sometimes used to represent a color in HTML coding. For example, the hex code for black is #000000 and for white is #FFFFFF.

hosted: A Web site housed on the blog software provider's servers.

HTML: Code used to create Web sites or parts of Web sites. The code, in the form of tags, often designates formatting of text or images on the Web page. For example, a paragraph is designated with the tag <p> at the beginning of the paragraph and </p> at the end of the paragraph. HTML stands for hypertext markup language.

HTML editor: An editing window in blog software where you can edit a blog post's HTML code. Some blog platforms provide both an HTML and a WYSIWYG (what you see is what you get) editor.

influencers: A term from the PR industry, used to describe bloggers and others highly visible on the Internet who have a wide readership and can influence the action of their readers by what they post.

link: Text or image coded so that when clicked on opens another Web page, either on the same or a different Web site.

link love: Linking to someone's blog or Web site when you mention that person in a blog post. This helps boost that person in search engine rankings.

linkback: *See* TRACKBACK.

linkbait: Linking to someone's blog in a blog post specifically for the purpose of having that person link back to the blog post. This is often done in the form of a long list of links to various blogs in an attempt to drive significant traffic to the blog post and drive the blog up in search engine ranking. Many bloggers consider this on par with spam.

linkroll: A list of links to Web sites or Web pages, usually found in the sidebar of some blogs. This is similar to a blogroll but includes sites other than blogs.

microblogging: Communication achieved in very short messages or posts, usually 140 characters in length. Made popular by the Web service Twitter; messages on Twitter are called "tweets."

moderation: An option allowed by most blog software platforms: comments are held privately for an administrator to review before releasing publicly to the blog. This gives the blog administrator a chance to delete or edit the comment before it goes "live" on the blog.

open source: Software or computer code free for use and modification by anyone, usually created by someone who volunteers. Probably the best known open source software is the Firefox Web browser created by the Mozilla community. The blog platform WordPress is also an open source project. Open source is abbreviated as OS.

OPML: An XML format for outlines, often used to create a special feed that contains a group of feeds and can be used to transfer a group of feeds from one aggregator to another. OPML stands for outline processor markup language.

permalink: A URL that links directly to an individual blog post. This is useful for directing readers to specific blog posts because over time those blog posts will roll off the blog's front page.

platform: A software framework that allows a software application to run. May also refer to the hardware or machinery on which the software runs.

plug-ins: Coding that gives features or functionality to software. WordPress blogs, for example, use a number of plug-ins created by the WordPress open source community.

podcast: A series of audio or video files that are syndicated using an RSS feed. Podcasts are made available through iTunes, other podcast providers, or individual podcast blogs. Listeners or viewers may subscribe to receive new episodes automatically through iTunes or another aggregator. The term "podcast" was created by combining the name "iPod" with the term "broadcast"; however, you do not need an iPod to listen to a podcast. They may be listened to or viewed on a computer or with any MP3 device, including iPods.

return on influence: A term from the social media PR industry describing the measurement of how much impact or influence a blog has, the number of other sites linking to the blog, as well as the number or quality of conversations about a blog or services taking place online. Abbreviated as ROI, it is meant to be a better measure of blog success than return on investment (also abbreviated as ROI).

RGB: Abbreviation of "Red Green Blue" and is a type of precise value scale for colors. The RGB value for black is 0,0,0 and for white is 255,255,255.

ROI: Traditionally stands for "return on investment" but in social media circles refers instead to "return on influence," which is perhaps the better measure to determine blog success. *See* RETURN ON INFLUENCE.

RSS: Feeds from blogs or other sources such as news sites or Google Alerts, coded in XML. These feeds can be read with an aggregator or fed onto a Web page for viewing. RSS stands for "really simple syndication." Atom is another, similar format.

screencasts: A video showing just a computer screen along with audio narration, usually used for instructional purposes to demonstrate software applications.

self-hosted: A Web site housed on the blog or Web site owner's own servers or housed on servers other than the blog software provider's.

sockpuppet: A fake ID or persona created by a troll to post comments on a blog, usually with a viewpoint sympathetic to the blog audience. The troll argues back and forth with the sockpuppet, trying to draw other readers in, thereby extending attention given to the troll.

tag cloud: A graphical representation of tags used on a Web site such as a blog. The tags are usually shown in either alphabetical order or by order of popularity. The tags used the most visually stand out more than tags used less; this is most often achieved by making popular tags larger and/or bolder.

tags: A Web 2.0–type feature, informal labels that may be applied to individual items on the Internet or an intranet such as blog posts, wiki pages, photographs, videos, bookmarks, or even catalog records. Tags may be applied either by the person who created the item or by the reader or viewer. While categories are formal and structured, tags are informal and unstructured. We label things in an ad hoc manner with tags, and different people will likely label things differently. While categories can give some hierarchical structure (as in a taxonomy), tags provide us with a more granular way to identify and locate items of interest such as blog posts. The term is also used in the programming world to describe some of the code in markup languages such as HTML and XML.

thumbnail: A small image file used to represent a larger image on the Internet. Usually clicking on a thumbnail image opens the larger image. This allows many images to be shown on a Web page while still allowing the page to load quickly in the browser.

trackback: Also known as a linkback, when another blog is linking to a specific post on your blog, and your blog shows that reference so that comments both on and off the blog are consolidated with their respective blog posts. Trackbacks are sometimes generated automatically; sometimes the blog software requires a special link to be added to create the relationship between blog posts.

trolls: Commenters purposely being negative and contrary to get a reaction from others. Trolling is usually an attention-seeking activity and done anonymously. While most trolls are harmless, some can be more malevolent and progress to stalker-type activities.

Web 2.0: A phrase coined in 1999 and made popular in 2004 to describe changes occurring on the Internet—a synergy created between what was then a new collection of technologies (AJAX) and a new attitude of people using the Internet marked by collaboration and more openness. This phrase is at times used interchangeably with the phrases "social media," "new media," and "social networking."

widgets: Little applications that can be attached to your blog (or other Web site) to do something very specific. Also known as "gadgets." Badges are a specific type of widget.

WYSIWYG editors: An editing window in blogging or other software that allows for editing without the use of HTML coding knowledge. Most e-mail and word processor software, for example, uses WYSIWYG editors. WYSIWYG stands for "what you see is what you get." Some blog platforms provide both a WYSIWYG and an HTML editor.

XML: The coding used for feeds. It uses tagging that looks similar to HTML coding; however, its tags denote function rather than format. For example, a blog post title might be coded with the tags <title> at the beginning and </title> at the end of the blog post. Aggregators and Web sites can then apply their own formatting or style to the text.

RECOMMENDED READING AND RESOURCES

▶ BLOGS, WEB SITES, AND PODCASTS

All Access Blogging. "How to Make Your Blog Accessible." Available: www
.allaccessblogging.com/make-your-blog-accessible.html (accessed February 2, 2010).

Blog Carnival. Available: http://blogcarnival.com/bc (accessed February 2, 2010).

The Blogging Libraries Wiki. Created and hosted by Amanda Etches-Johnson. Available: www.blogwithoutalibrary.net/links/index.php?title=Welcome_to_the_Blogging_Libraries_Wiki (accessed February 2, 2010).

David Lee King. Created and hosted by David Lee King. Available: www
.davidleeking.com (accessed February 2, 2010).

Finding Library Weblogs. Compiled by Darlene Fichter. Available: http://
library2.usask.ca/~fichter/weblog/library_weblogs.html (accessed February 2, 2010).

Google Basics: Webmasters Tools Help. Available: www.google.com/support/
webmasters/bin/answer.py?answer=70897 (accessed February 2, 2010).

Google Gadgets for Your Webpage. Available: www.google.com/ig/directory
?synd=open (accessed February 2, 2010).

Groundswell. Created and hosted by Forrester Research. Available: www
.forrester.com/Groundswell (accessed February 2, 2010).

In the Library with the Lead Pipe. Available: http://inthelibrarywiththelead
pipe.org (accessed February 2, 2010).

Influx Blog. Created and hosted by Aaron Schmidt and Amanda Etches-Johnson. Available: http://influx.us/blog (accessed February 2, 2010).

Librarian Blogs and Sites Internet Directory. Available: http://librariansindex
.blogspot.com (accessed February 2, 2010).

Library Blogging. Available: http://libraryblogging.com (accessed February 2, 2010).

LIBWorm. Available: www.libworm.com (accessed February 2, 2010).

LISWiki—Weblogs. Available: http://liswiki.org/wiki/Blogs (accessed February 2, 2010).

LISZen. Available: http://liszen.com (accessed February 2, 2010).

Marketing Over Coffee (podcast). Available: www.marketingovercoffee.com (accessed February 2, 2010).

Meebo Me. Available: www.meebome.com (accessed February 2, 2010).

My Kansas Library on the Web. Available: www.mykansaslibrary.org (accessed February 2, 2010).

ProBlogger. Available: www.problogger.net (accessed February 2, 2010).

ReCAPTCHA. Available: http://recaptcha.net (accessed February 2, 2010).

Slideshare. Available: www.slideshare.net (accessed February 2, 2010).

Smashing Magazine. Available: www.smashingmagazine.com (accessed February 2, 2010).

TED Talks. Available: www.ted.com (accessed February 2, 2010).

U.S. Department of Health and Human Services. "Research-Based Web Design & Usability Guidelines." Available: www.usability.gov/pdfs/guidelines.html (accessed February 2, 2010).

W3C Web Accessibility Initiative. Available: www.w3.org/WAI (accessed February 2, 2010).

WebAIM. "Introduction to Web Accessibility." Available: www.webaim.org/intro (accessed February 2, 2010).

Webcredible. "Web Accessibility Articles." Available: www.webcredible.co.uk/user-friendly-resources/web-accessibility (accessed February 2, 2010).

Weblog Tools Collection. Available: http://weblogtoolscollection.com (accessed February 2, 2010).

Widgetbox. Available: www.widgetbox.com (accessed February 2, 2010).

WordPress TV. Available: http://wordpress.tv (accessed February 2, 2010).

► ARTICLES, BLOG POSTS, AND PRESENTATIONS

Agarwal, Amit. "Increase Your Blog's RSS Subscriber Count with Bloglines Tools." Digital Inspiration, April 10, 2008. Available: www.labnol.org/internet/blogging/increase-blog-rss-subscriber-count-feedburner-bloglines/2913 (accessed February 2, 2010).

Agrawal, Harsh. "8 Reasons Why Self Hosted WordPress Blog Is Better Than Blogspot Blog." Shout Me Loud, April 21, 2009. Available: www.shoutmeloud.com/8-reasons-why-self-hosted-wordpress-blog-is-better-than-blogspot-blog.html (accessed February 2, 2010).

Aylward, Kevin. "Blogrolls Are so 2004. . . ." Wizbang, July 11, 2009. Available: http://wizbangblog.com/content/2009/07/11/blogrolls-are-so-2004.php (accessed February 2, 2010).

Bauer, Elise. "Backing Up Your Blog." Learning Movable Type, July 19, 2004. Available: www.learningmovabletype.com/a/000587backing_up_blog (accessed February 2, 2010).

Brazell, Aaron. "Tag, You're It! Leveraging Tagging for Your Blog" (guest post under Darren Rowse' name). ProBlogger, February 27, 2006. Available: www.problogger.net/archives/2006/02/27/tag-youre-it-leveraging-tagging -for-your-blog (accessed February 2, 2010).

Brogan, Chris. "20 Blog Topics to Get You Unstuck." Chris Brogan, March 17, 2009. Available: www.chrisbrogan.com/20-blog-topics-to-get-you-unstuck (accessed February 2, 2010).

Chitu, Alex. "The Number of iGoogle/Google Reader Subscribers." Google Operating System, September 15, 2007. Available: http://googlesystem .blogspot.com/2007/09/number-of-igoogle-google-reader.html (accessed February 2, 2010).

Cohen, Sarah Faye. "Exploring New Technology 4: Feevy." The Sheck Spot, May 17, 2007. Available: http://theshecksspot.blogspot.com/2007/05/ exploring-new-technology-4-feevy.html (accessed February 2, 2010).

Curtis, Jason. "Creating a Library Blog." Presentation posted to Slideshare, April 26, 2007. Available: www.slideshare.net/sathlibraries/creating-a-library-blog-with-blogger (accessed February 2, 2010).

Deschamps, Ryan. "Search Engine Optimization (SEO) Tips for Libraries." The Other Librarian, July 14, 2008. Available: http://otherlibrarian .wordpress.com/2008/07/14/search-engine-optimization-seo-tips-for-libraries (accessed February 2, 2010).

———. "Three Briefs about Your Web Presence." The Other Librarian, July 26, 2008. Available: http://otherlibrarian.wordpress.com/2008/07/26/ three-briefs-about-your-web-presence (accessed February 2, 2010).

Dick, Jason. "What Makes a Cookie a Spyware Cookie?" StopSign, September 5, 2007. Available: http://home.stopsign.com/reference/articles/what-makes-a-cookie-a-spyware-cookie.php (accessed February 2, 2010).

Escala Web Strategy. "20 Things to Check before Buying a WordPress Theme." Available: http://escalawebstrategy.com/web/20-things-to-check-before-buying-a-wordpress-theme (accessed February 2, 2010).

Etches-Johnson, Amanda. "Ten Tips to Market Your Library Blog." PowerPoint presented at BlogU, September 18, 2005. Available: www .blogwithoutalibrary.net/talk/blogu/marketingtentips.ppt (accessed February 2, 2010).

Farrelly, Glen. "Help Getting Started with Web Accessibility." Webslinger, March 29, 2009. Available: http://glenfarrelly.blogspot.com/2009/ 03/help-getting-started-with-web.html (accessed February 2, 2010).

Fichter, Darlene. "Widgets, Tools, and Doodads for Library Webmasters." Computers in Libraries 2008, April 7, 2008. Available: www.slideshare .net/fichter/widgets-tools-and-doodads-for-webmasters (accessed February 2, 2010).

Germsheid, Cassie. "Google Analytics versus Statcounter." Mamas on the Web, March 24, 2009. Available: http://mamasontheweb.com/2009/03/24/google-analytics-versus-statcounter (accessed February 2, 2010).

Goetz, Michele. "Timing Is a Critical Success Factor for Blog Posts." Social Media Today, July 3, 2009. Available: www.socialmediatoday.com/SMC/106788 (accessed February 2, 2010).

Google. "Corporation Information: Technology Overview." Available: www .google.com/corporate/tech.html (accessed February 2, 2010).

Herrman, Kathy. "Why Squarespace Is a Super Blogging Platform." Intellicore Design Consulting, April 2, 2009. Available: http://community .intellicore-design.com/blog/2009/4/2/why-squarespace-is-a-super-blogging-platform.html (accessed February 2, 2010).

Hunsucker, Maggie. "Hip to Be Square: Build a Well-Designed, Feature-Rich Site with Hosted Content Manager Squarespace." feed growth!, December 29, 2008. Available: http://feedgrowth.com/idea-categories/blogging-and-publishing/build-a-well-designed-feature-rich-site-with-hosted-content-manager-squarespace (accessed February 2, 2010).

King, David Lee. "Fun with Our Meebo Widget and the Library Catalog." David Lee King, November 30, 2007. Available: www.davidleeking.com/2007/11/30/fun-with-our-meebo-widget-and-the-library-catalog (accessed February 2, 2010).

———. "More Chat in the Catalog." David Lee King, May 30, 2009. Available: www.davidleeking.com/2009/05/30/more-chat-in-the-catalog (accessed February 2, 2010).

Kirkpatrick, Marshall. "Want That Post to Go Popular? Here's the Best and the Worst Times to Post It." ReadWriteWeb, May 2, 2008. Available: www.readwriteweb.com/archives/new_study_shows_best_and_worst.php (accessed February 2, 2010).

Kroski, Ellyssa. "Folksonomies and Social Tagging Presentation Video." Infotangle, July 4, 2007; presented at Library 2.0 Conference, Ohio State University Libraries, June 14, 2007. Available: http://infotangle.blogsome .com/2007/07/04/folksonomies-and-social-tagging-presentation-video (accessed February 2, 2010).

———. "The Hive Mind: Folksonomies and User-Based Tagging." Infotangle, December 7, 2005. Available: http://infotangle.blogsome.com/2005/12/07/the-hive-mind-folksonomies-and-user-based-tagging (accessed February 2, 2010).

———. "How to Create a Mobile Website for Your Blog." iLibrarian, October 23, 2006. Available: http://oedb.org/blogs/ilibrarian/2008/how-to-create-a-mobile-website-for-your-blog (accessed February 2, 2010).

Kwong, Vincci and Julie Elliott. "Using Blogs, MySpace, and Facebook to Promote Your Library." PowerPoint presented at Librarians Day 2007, June 1, 2007. Available: www.indiana.edu/~iulfc/presentation/Blogs.ppt (accessed February 2, 2010).

Lang, Kathy. "Writing for International Readers." Writing for the World. Available: www.writingworldwide.com (accessed February 2, 2010).

Le, Vinh. "How to Blog Design Style Guide." Blog Design Blog, April 15, 2008. Available: www.blogdesignblog.com/blog-design/how-to-blog-design-style-guide (accessed February 2, 2010).

Martin, Michael. "Using Categories and Tags Effectively on Your Blog." ProBlogger (guest post under Darren Rowse' name), September 27, 2007. Available: www.problogger.net/archives/2007/09/27/using-categories-and-tags-effectively-on-your-blog (accessed February 2, 2010).

Matthews, Steve. "The Hub-n-wheel Strategy." Law Firm Web Strategy Blog, August 2, 2007. Available: www.stemlegal.com/strategyblog/2007/the-hub-n-wheel-strategy (accessed February 2, 2010).

McMahon, Thomas. "How Do You Backup a Blog?" bloggerdesign, April 13, 2006. Available: http://bloggerdesign.com/44/how-do-you-backup-a-blog (accessed February 2, 2010).

Morin, Rita. "Cool Tools Episode 44 Podcast: Weebly." Cool Tools for Library 2.0, April 9, 2009. Available: http://cooltoolslibrary2.blogspot.com/2009/04/cool-tools-episode-44-podcast-weebly.html (accessed February 2, 2010).

Odom, Eric. "Did Sitemeter Sell Out to Spyware?" Eric Odom, March 26, 2007. Available: http://conservablogs.com/EricOdom/2007/03/26/did-sitemeter-sell-out-to-spyware (accessed February 2, 2010).

———. "Sitemeter Responds." Eric Odom, April 5, 2007. Available: http://conservablogs.com/EricOdom/2007/04/05/sitemeter-responds (accessed February 2, 2010).

O'Driscoll, Sean. "The Trouble with Trolls." Ant's Eye View, June 7, 2007. Available: www.antseyeview.com/blog/197/the-trouble-with-trolls (accessed February 2, 2010).

Oleson, Joel. "What Makes a Good Blog?" SharePoint Joel, July 18, 2008. Available: www.sharepointjoel.com/Lists/Posts/Post.aspx?ID=64 (accessed February 2, 2010).

Pacifici, Sabrina. "Competitive Intelligence—A Selective Resource Guide." LLRX.com, first published November 20, 2005; updated and revised March 2009. Available: www.llrx.com/features/ciguide.htm (accessed February 2, 2010).

———. "Leveraging Blogs, RSS, News Alerts and Different Search Engines to Expand Your Research." LLRX.com, November 22, 2006. Available: www.llrx.com/features/expandresearch.htm [PDF] (accessed February 2, 2010).

Paulson, Matthew. "Using BlogCarnivals to Promote Your Blog." AC Associated Content January 30, 2007. Available: www.associatedcontent.com/article/128305/using_blogcarnivals_to_promote_your.html (accessed February 2, 2010).

RawVoice. "Blogging and Podcasting Terms." podcastFAQ. Available: www.podcastfaq.com/glossary/blogging-and-podcasting-terms (accessed February 2, 2010).

Robledo, Colleen. "Redesigned My Blog." Colleen's Commentary, July 2, 2009. Available: www.colleenscommentary.net/2009/07/02/redesigned-my-blog (accessed February 2, 2010).

Rowse, Darren. "8 First Step SEO Tips for Bloggers." ProBlogger, July 2, 2009. Available: www.problogger.net/archives/2009/07/02/seo-tips-for-bloggers (accessed February 2, 2010).

Samuel, Colin. "Blawg Review #35." Infamy or Praise, December 5, 2005. Available: http://infamyorpraise.blogspot.com/2005/12/blawg-review-35.html (accessed February 2, 2010).

Schroeder, Stan. "50 Great Widgets for Your Blog." Mashable, September 6, 2007. Available: http://mashable.com/2007/09/06/widgets-2 (accessed February 2, 2010).

Scocco, Daniel. "Backup Your Blog Regularly." DailyBlogtips, July 13, 2007. Available: www.dailyblogtips.com/backup-your-blog-regularly (accessed February 2, 2010).

Smith, Aaron. "New Numbers for Blogging and Blog Readership." Pew Internet & American Life Project, July 22, 2008. Available: www.pewinternet.org/Commentary/2008/July/New-numbers-for-blogging-and-blog-readership.aspx (accessed February 2, 2010).

Tucker, Christy. "Hunting for Subscribers Stats." Experience E-Learning, January 17, 2008. Available: http://christytucker.wordpress.com/2008/01/17/hunting-for-subscriber-stats (accessed February 2, 2010).

Weinberger, David. "Whitehouse.gov: Name Your Bloggers!" The Huffington Post, May 16, 2009. Available: www.huffingtonpost.com/david-weinberger/whitehousegov-name-your-b_b_204265.html (accessed February 2, 2010).

Wilhelm, Alex. "Squarespace v. WordPress—The Best Blogging Platform." The Mind of Alex, March 3, 2009. Available: http://alexwilhelm.com/2009/03/03/squarespace-v-wordpress-the-best-blogging-platform (accessed February 2, 2010).

WindowsObserver. "Five Blogroll Plugins for Your WordPress Site." Weblog Tools Collection, June 4, 2009. Available: http://weblogtoolscollection.com/archives/2009/06/04/five-blogroll-plugins-for-your-wordpress-site (accessed February 2, 2010).

Wynne, Angela. "Sitemeter vs. StatCounter: Why I Prefer StatCounter." BlogCoach, July 21, 2008. Available: www.blogcoach.org/2008/06/ sitemeter-vs-statcounter.html (accessed February 2, 2010).

▶ BOOKS

Coombs, Karen A. and Jason Griffey. 2008. *Library Blogging*. Santa Barbara: Linworth Books.

Crawford, Walt. 2009. *The Liblog Landscape 2007–2008: A Lateral Look*. Cites & Insights, 2009. Available: www.lulu.com/content/paperback-book/ the-liblog-landscape-2007-2008/4898086.

King, David Lee. 2008. *Designing the Digital Experience: How to Use Experience Design Tools & Techniques to Build Websites Customers Love*. Medford, NJ: Information Today, CyberAge Books,.

Li, Charlene and Josh Bernoff. 2008. *Groundswell: Winning in a World Transformed by Social Technologies*. Boston: Harvard Business School Press.

Sauers, Michael P. 2007. *Blogging and RSS: A Librarian's Guide*. Medford, NJ: Information Today.

Scoble, Robert and Shel Israel. 2006. *Naked Conversations: How Blogs Are Changing the Way Businesses Talk with Customers*. New York: Wiley.

INDEX

Page numbers followed by the letter "f" indicate figures.